DECEPTIV

Printed in the United States of America by Market Source, INC.

Cover graphics by Brandy Spain

Copyright © 2010 by Gary G. Tavares

Gary G. Tavares

Tavares Entertainment, LLC.

903-B Honey Creek Rd. #186

Conyers, GA 30094

678-437-4496

docperformer@hotmail.com

www.tavaresentertainment.net

ISBN: 978-0-615-40073-0

ACKNOWLEGEMENTS

First of all I would like to thank the good Lord for giving me this talent. He has made me a strong man and he has instilled in me a, "Save the world" mentality.

There are so many people who have come into my life and inspired me. Far too many for me to remember or thank. I would rather just thank everyone who has been instrumental in getting me to this place where I am now.

Thanks go to my siblings for empowering me with the passion and the vision to strive to be my best.

Thanks to the military, Navy and Army, for teaching me to overcome and adapt.

Thank you Lester Wright, Educator, for taking time out of your busy schedule to help me tighten this book up. Your tireless support and time for this and many of my projects, is much appreciated.

Thank you Robert, Lawyer, for your countless hours giving me your expert legal opinion on various scenes and scenarios throughout the book. You helped me make the story more believable, even though it is fictitious.

Thank you Ariel Glover, Singer/Songwriter, for just sitting down with me and giving me words of encouragement from time to time.

Thank you Borders Books of Stone crest Mall in Lithonia, Georgia. Your managers and staff are very professional and know how to treat authors and artists.

DEDICATED TO:

This book is dedicated to ALL victims of domestic violence and abuse, past and present. May you find the courage to move on and the strength to overcome the problems caused by the abuse. For those who are being abused presently, may this book give you the courage to seek and find help before it is too late.

INTRODUCTION

Deceptive Vows is a powerful, thought-provoking and educational novel that addresses the issue of domestic violence. It is based on the play written and directed by Gary G. Tavares entitled, "Until Death Do Us Part." The play was performed in Oakland California in 2000 and brought back for an encore presentation in 2001. The Screenplay version was also written by Gary G. Tavares. The Screenplay was completed in 2005 and is also entitled, Deceptive Vows.

The purpose of the novel is to bring awareness to the issue of domestic violence and possibly save lives. A portion of the proceeds will be donated to a domestic violence shelter or organization of the author's choice.

Prevalence of Domestic Violence

- In a 1995-1996 study conducted in the 50 States and the District of Columbia, nearly 25% of women and 7.6% of men were raped and/or physically assaulted by a current or former spouse, cohabiting partner, or dating partner/acquaintance at some time in their lifetime (based on survey of 16,000 participants, equally male and female).

  Patricia Tjaden & Nancy Thoennes, U.S. Dep't of Just., NCJ 181867, *Extent, Nature, and Consequences of Intimate Partner Violence, at iii (2000),* available at http://www.ojp.usdoj.gov/nij/pubs-sum/181867.htm

- Approximately 1.3 million women and 835,000 men are physically assaulted by an intimate partner annually in the United States.

  Patricia Tjaden & Nancy Thoennes, U.S. Dep't of Just., NCJ 183781, *Full Report of the Prevalence, Incidence, and Consequences of Intimate Partner Violence Against Women: Findings from the National Violence Against Women Survey, at iv* (2000), available at http://www.ojp.usdoj.gov/nij/pubs-sum/183781.htm

- Intimate partner violence made up 20% of all nonfatal violent crime experienced by women in 2001.

  Callie Marie Rennison, U.S. Dep't of Just., NCJ 197838, Bureau of Justice Statistics Crime Data Brief: Intimate Partner Violence, 1993-2001, at 1 (2003), available at http://www.ojp.usdoj.gov/bjs/pub/pdf/ipv01.pdf

- Intimate partners committed 3% of the nonfatal violent crimes against men.

  Callie Marie Rennison, U.S. Dep't of Just., NCJ 197838, *Bureau of Justice Statistics Crime Data Brief: Intimate Partner Violence, 1993-2001, at 1* (2003), available at http://www.ojp.usdoj.gov/bjs/pub/pdf/ipv01.pdf

- In 2000, 1,247 women and 440 men were killed by an intimate partner. In recent years, an intimate partner killed approximately 33% of female murder victims and 4% of male murder victims.

  Callie Marie Rennison, U.S. Dep't of Just., NCJ 197838, *Bureau of Justice Statistics Crime Data Brief: Intimate Partner Violence, 1993-2001, at 1* (2003), available at http://www.ojp.usdoj.gov/bjs/pub/pdf/ipv01.pdf

- Access to firearms yields a more than five-fold increase in risk of intimate partner homicide when considering other factors of abuse, according to a recent study, suggesting that abusers who possess guns tend to inflict the most severe abuse on their partners.

Jacquelyn C. Campbell et al., *Risk Factors For Femicide in Abusive Relationships: Results From A Multi-Site Case Control Study, 93 Am. J. of Public Health 1089, 1092 (2003)*, abstract available at http://www.ajph.org/cgi/content/abstract/93/7/1089

- Of females killed with firearms, almost two-thirds were killed by their intimate partners. The number of females shot and killed by their husband or intimate partner was more than three times higher than the total number murdered by male strangers using all weapons combined in single victim/single offender incidents in 2002.

The Violence Pol'y Ctr., *When Men Murder Women: An Analysis of 2002 Homicide Data: Females Murdered by Males in Single Victim/Single Offender Incidents, at 7 (2004)*, available at http://www.vpc.org/studies/wmmw2004.pdf

According to the U.S. Department of Justice, between 1998 and 2002:

- Of the almost 3.5 million violent crimes committed against family members, 49% of these were crimes against spouses.
- 84% of spouse abuse victims were females, and 86% of victims of dating partner abuse were female.

- Males were 83% of spouse murderers and 75% of dating partner murderers
- 50% of offenders in state prison for spousal abuse had killed their victims.
- Wives were more likely than husbands to be killed by their spouses: wives were about half of all spouses in the population in 2002, but 81% of all persons killed by their spouse.

Matthew R. Durose et al., U.S. Dep't of Just., NCJ 207846, *Bureau of Justice Statistics, Family Violence Statistics: Including Statistics on Strangers and Acquaintances, at 31-32 (2005)*, available at http://www.ojp.usdoj.gov/bjs/pub/pdf/fvs.pdf

BATTERED AND BRUISED

You're trying your best to hide your bruises.

He slaps you around and says that you're useless.

You're starting to believe that maybe it's true.

He doesn't appreciate anything you do.

Make-up hides bruises but not the pain.

There's little sunshine and lots of rain.

It's like you're on a Roller Coaster ride,

with Doctor Jekyll and Mister Hyde.

Love should never include pain.

but for you he has so much disdain.

You say it's hard for you to get out,

could it be yourself who you really doubt?

Being beat by him is not amusing,

he tells you he loves you but it's you he's confusing.

Everyone wonders why you keep on staying,

you'll get out safely we're hoping and praying.

He keeps getting worse and acting real strange,

when will you realize he's not going to change?

The verbal abuse is just as bad,

It tears you down and keeps you sad.

It makes you feel like less than a lady,

and sometimes it even makes you feel crazy.

What he did to you was assault and battery,

you keep on saying, "Oh he's just mad at me."

You keep on believing that it's your fault,

and you keep on taking his assault.

The police come so often your home is their substation;

you never press charges so it causes frustration.

Sad thing is he too was a victim,

but I refuse to make excuses for him.

Just take a look at your face in the mirror,

old bruises new bruises but it never gets clearer.

Sometimes he treats you like you're a Queen,

but what about the times he's just plain mean?

You long for the times he treats you right,

you're hoping and praying for another good night.

Please get out of this for heaven's sake,

If you don't you're making a big mistake.

When all is said and done it's your decision,

getting out should be your primary mission.

You thought he was the best man in the world,

but you made a mistake so move on girl!

CHAPTER ONE

****

Patricia Robinson lies in her prison bed staring into space. She is a medium-sized black female, in her late twenties. Her hair is shoulder-length and braided to the back. She has on blue, prison issue overalls. Her number is stenciled on the front of the overalls and Hanford Woman's Correctional Facility is on the back. The cell is small with a bunk bed and toilet. Patricia does not have a cell mate. She has several pictures of her mother, father, friends and her now two-year old son Marcus.

A rather large Caucasian female guard runs a stick along the metal bars to get Patricia's attention. Patricia just moaned as she lied there in the fetal position. The female guard opened Patricia's cell. She stood there waiting for Patricia.

She said, "It is time for your group therapy session young lady. The other inmates as well as the doctor are waiting for you."

"I told you all I don't need no stupid therapy!" Patricia shouted.

The guard looked at Patricia and said, "I will not put up with your mess under any circumstances. Now you know I am not the one!"

Patricia jumped up as if a fire alarm went off. She knew better than to test her luck with this particular guard. She was pretty big and mean and known to do some attitude adjusting. Patricia stormed out of her cell. The female guard caught up to Patricia and escorted her to the class. There were ten women sitting at a group of tables that were brought together. At the head of the table is a gentleman peering over his glasses. The gentleman's name is Doctor Morgan, who is highly trusted and respected by all the inmates. He is a black man, in his mid to late fifties. He has a pretty thick goatee and wears fairly thick glasses.

The women who have recently started serving time are easily noticed. Many of them have fresh cuts and bruises from abusive relationships. Counting Patricia, there are six black female inmates and five white female inmates present. The room was painted an awful green color. The guard sat Patricia down and continued to stand over her. There are three other pretty big female guards at the session. One is Caucasian and the other two are black.

"Patricia we are all glad you were able to make it," Doctor Morgan said with a somewhat sarcastic tone.

Patricia mumbled, "I can't stand this shit!"

The large white guard said, "Behave young lady or I will lock your ass up in solitary confinement!"

Doctor Morgan put his glasses on the table. He shook his head and wiped the sweat off his forehead with a handkerchief.

He told the guards, "Everything is okay and the situation here is under control."

After all, Doctor Morgan did have an image and a reputation with these women that included trust. The prison guard did back off Patricia but very slowly. Patricia did not seem to be threatened by the guard. Patricia's mean cold stare down of the guard was quite intense.

Surprisingly, Doctor Morgan said, "All the guards in here are free to leave."

He did not want things to escalate.

One of the black female guards said, "Doctor Morgan we do not believe you are safe here with the inmates alone."

Doctor Morgan felt safe because he had never been physically attacked by an inmate in all his years in the system. The guards would be standing right outside the door at all times, watching the inmates through the glass pane in the door.

After the four guards left, Dr. Morgan flipped through his papers and said, "It looks like we are up to Carol Witherspoon. Remember, we are all like friends and family here. No matter what happens outside this room, we are family here. The one thing that connects all of you is your past and your experiences with domestic violence. So, we are not here to judge each other. In a way, I guess you help each other by sharing your experiences."

Doctor Morgan took several boxes of tissues from his bag and passed them around the table. There was never a shortage of tissue boxes at these sessions.

Doctor Morgan peered around the table and said, "Okay we will start with Carol and work our way around the table."

Carol was a rather small black woman, in her early to mid-fifties. She had a notable scar on her face from past abuse. Carol pulled a box of tissues next to her. She was nearly in tears before she even began to tell her story. The other inmates just listened and stared at Carol. It was so quiet you could probably hear a pin drop. Carol was one of the more senior women in the group so she received quite a bit more attention.

Carol finally choked forth the words and said, "I am here for killing my abusive husband John. I met him about four years ago in San Francisco. We got married after dating about three months. At first he appeared to be the best man a woman could have. About a month into the marriage he started physically and mentally abusing me. One night he got home drunk and started beating me. I had a nine-year old son named Kevin from a previous marriage. He came out to protect me and John started beating him like a man. I was used to the beatings but I never saw John strike Kevin before. I guess I became like a female bear protecting its cub. I ran into Kevin's room and got his Louisville Slugger baseball bat. I beat John until he was motionless. I thought I knocked him out but when the Paramedics came they started doing CPR on John. He died later at the hospital from massive blunt force trauma to the head and skull fractures."

Several of the women in the session needed to pass the box of tissues around during this frightening story. Even the doctor seemed to dislike what he was hearing. Doctor Morgan asked a somewhat critical question. He was known to ask tough questions at the sessions.

He asked, "Why did you stay in the abusive relationship?"

At first Carol and the other women looked at the doctor as if he was crazy.

However, Carol did answer the question by saying, "I stayed married to John for five hellish years because I thought John would change or that maybe I could change him. Another reason was that I was afraid. My family lived clear across the country on the east coast, and I didn't really have any friends. I also had a son to think about. I kept wondering where we would go and how would I provide for Kevin and myself. I did not have any skills and I never had to work before. Moreover, my husband was the sole provider. So, basically I was afraid to step out on my own."

Doctor Morgan looked around and asked, "How do we stop the cycle of violence? I mean, what are some of the things you believe would help?"

That was a question he was sure to ask each session. Sharon Walker, a rather petite black female in her thirties, looked around for a second. All eyes were on her because she was next.

Sharon said, "Okay I guess I'm up now, so I will tell my story.

In my case my husband just refused to let me go. He just kept on stalking me.

I tried everything to escape him. I even moved countless times. No matter where I went he would find me. Hell a restraining order was not even worth the ink and paper it used. By the time the police got there he was always long gone, and there was no way to prove he harassed me. I blame the judicial system for not doing enough."

Doctor Morgan scribbled some notes down, pushed his glasses up on his face and scratched his head.

He cleared his throat and proceeded to say, "So you believe the judicial system fails to do enough to stop this problem, right?"

Sharon Walker shook her head yes and went on to say, "One time my husband punched me in the eye. I had a black eye, which was swollen almost shut. Sacramento's finest came and took my husband away for assault and battery. Believe it or not he was back out in less than seventy-two hours. I got sick of the physical and verbal abuse and left him. However, he simply refused to let me live in peace. As I said, He always would find me eventually. I feel the police were of little help to me and my situation. He should not have been able to continue to stalk me, harass me and abuse me.

I felt the only way to get peace was to take him out. So that is what I did. I pretended to take him back. I even moved back in with him. I took his abuse because I had a plan. My plan was to poison him to death. I started poisoning him and he died about two or three days later."

Sharon snatched up the box of tissues and wiped her tears.

Carol Witherspoon tried to comfort her and said, "It is okay Sharon you can do this. Just let it go girl and you will feel a lot better."

Sharon continued and said, "Since I went after him it was called premeditated murder. Sad thing is I do not regret killing him. I knew he would never stalk or abuse me again. I have done ten years now and I still do not regret killing him. I just regret doing time for it."

Sharon paused for a minute and said, "By the way I didn't say my name. I am Sharon Walker."

Doctor Morgan shook his head again and then spoke. He said, "Thank you Sharon and Carol for sharing your stories. Your stories were remarkable and powerful. Okay, it looks like we have time for one more story. Patricia we are up to you."

Patricia just sat there looking around for a few seconds and said, "I pass!"

Doctor Morgan said, "Patricia are you sure you want to pass?"

"Yes Doctor Morgan I am sure! I don't have anything to say!" Patricia said a little more loudly.

Carol Witherspoon stood up and said, "Ladies, you are not going to help your situation by holding on to the pain you feel."

Patricia said, "Will you people just leave me alone? I said I don't want to do this. Why can't you fucking people understand that?"

Sharon Walker attempted to add to Carol's comment and said, "Girl you just need to...."

Doctor Morgan cleared his throat, interrupted her and said, "We can't force anyone here to talk."

Sharon Walker just fanned Patricia off and said, "Fine, it is her life!"

Patricia jumped across the table and grabbed Sharon by her throat.

She choked Sharon and yelled, "You don't even know me bitch!"

Suddenly, all four prison guards rushed into the room and separated Patricia and Sharon. They put some sort of restraints on Patricia and Sharon and escorted both of them out.

One of the black Guards looked at Doctor Morgan and said, "So Doctor Morgan, now you know why we prefer to stay in here."

Dr. Morgan sat there with a puzzled look for a second or two and said, "I am sort of in shock myself because this is the first time this ever happened."

The larger of the black guards said, "We intend to make sure it never happens again. Not on our watch! I do not care if you have to do the sessions in their cells. The session for today is now officially over and the women need to move out. Let's go ladies; stand up and move out!"

Dr. Morgan stood up as the women were all being marched out of the room and said, "I hope we can continue the session tomorrow."

CHAPTER TWO

****

Patricia tossed and turned in her bed. She was having a nightmare about her husband Andre. Andre approached Patricia. He had a very mean expression. Patricia began to back up slowly, but ended up in a corner. As her husband got close, she put her arms up to protect her face. It was not unusual for Patricia to have these recurring nightmares about her now deceased husband. Sometimes, like that night, she would wake up out of her sleep screaming or crying out loudly.

Patricia then woke up suddenly and shouted, "No, don't hurt me! I will do whatever you want!"

An Inmate from one of the adjacent cells yelled back at Patricia. She was not too happy about having her sleep disturbed by Patricia's screams.

She yelled out to Patricia, "Girl what the hell is wrong with you? Are you crazy or something?"

A guard's voice echoed through the prison as she said, "Cell block "C" ladies need to hold down the noise!"

The next morning a large black female guard brought Patricia to Dr. Morgan's office. This time Patricia had on the wrist and leg restraints.

Doctor Morgan straightened up his desk and said, "Please take the restraints off her."

The Guard looked at Doctor Morgan with disbelief and asked him, "Are you sure you want me to do this?"

The incident with Patricia, which happened only twenty-four hours earlier, should have been fresh in his mind. Usually Doctor Morgan leaned in favor of the inmates. He could identify with them to a certain degree and felt sympathetic towards them.

The guard unshackled Patricia but then put the restraints back on and said, "Doctor I think I better leave them on. Trust me you will be glad I did. I just don't trust this one."

The Doctor really did not believe Patricia would give him any more problems. He thought that if he could gain Patricia's trust it would be easier to communicate with her.

He wanted Patricia to drop her guard and open up to him. He felt it would be a little more difficult for her to open up and connect with him while she was tied up in restraints.

The guard said, "I am sorry Doctor Morgan but it's for your own safety. I'll be right outside in case you have any problems with her."

She turned to Patricia and gave her a mean look and said, "As for you young lady, don't you dare start no shit in here!"

The guard turned to walk outside. Patricia sucked her teeth and flipped off the guard once the guard turned her back. Patricia could not stand the guards and it seemed like they did not mind putting her in her place. Patricia did not feel she belonged there so she had a lot of anger.

Doctor Morgan said, "Hello Patricia."

Patricia did not respond, but she did look around the room. She refused to give him eye contact because she knew how he could almost mesmerize you with his looks. Patricia was one of the only inmates Doctor Morgan had not cracked. He felt it would just be a matter of time. Patricia looked down at a picture that was sitting on Doctor Morgan's desk. The picture was of Dr. Morgan, his wife, his daughter and his son. She stared at it for a while.

All Patricia wanted was to meet "Mister Right," start a family and live happily ever after. Needless to say, her marriage was in no way the fairy tale she had hoped for. After all, she never got to see herself, her husband Andre and their child in a photo together.

Doctor Morgan started the conversation off by saying, "Patricia nobody is going to force you to talk about your story. If you do not want to talk about what happened to you it is fine. Needless to say, telling your story could be beneficial to you."

Patricia examined the picture for a few more seconds. She then asked, "Is this your family?"

Doctor Morgan said, "It is my wife Julie, my son Jerry and my daughter Cheryl. Why are you asking about my family?"

He felt somewhat threatened and he felt she was being a bit intrusive.

"I don't know I guess I am curious," Patricia said as tears start to appear in her eyes.

It made her see what could have been her own family. Doctor Morgan removed the picture from the top of his desk and put it inside one of the desk drawers.

He did not want anything distracting or upsetting Patricia. He needed her to be focused on the session and he wanted her full attention. He wanted to get straight to the point.

"I brought you here to tell you that I may have to release you from the sessions. I simply cannot let one person destroy this program. There has been too much success in other facilities with the program," he said as he peered over his glasses.

Patricia got angry and said, "I will be stuck in this hell hole for a longer time if you release me from the damn program!"

"I don't have anything to do with that," said Doctor Morgan as he shrugged his shoulders and leaned back in his seat.

"Doctor Morgan what do you want from me?"

She really did not want to tell her story. Unfortunately, that was not what the state wanted. The state believed there has to be some sort of rehabilitation and intervention for any woman who has gone through what these women went through. They mandate the program and frankly Doctor Morgan agreed with them. Even though the program was fairly new it still was showing positive results in other facilities. Some inmates who completed the course did much better when they were released. In fact, some were able to be released earlier after completing the therapy program.

"Okay fine! I will go through the session, but I do not want to do it with the other inmates yet," Patricia said with an attitude.

Actually, Doctor Morgan was surprised at such a simple request. He did not care how or where Patricia told her story. Perhaps this was the break he was looking for. He knew if he agreed to this he could get her to tell her story.

Doctor Morgan scribbled down some more notes and then said, "So, basically you would like to have private sessions, right?"

Patricia shook her head yes as Doctor Morgan paused to think.

He looked up at the ceiling, twirled his goatee with his fingertips and said, "I can't make any guarantees but I promise to see what I can do. Now, In exchange, you need to promise me there will be no more outbursts or violent behavior. I also want you to promise to tell your story to the group. I am making an appointment for you to come back next Friday to tell me your story. Now, this is the last-ditch effort to rehabilitate you and get you through the state mandated program. There will be a heavy guard presence around you and the sessions, due to your unruly behavior. So, do you have any questions young lady?"

Patricia had one more question for Doctor Morgan. With his family's picture still fresh on her mind, she asked, "How old is your little boy?"

Once again he seemed reluctant and hesitant to talk about his family with an inmate.

However, he did say, "My baby boy is eighteen months old. Now I am reminding you once more of our Friday appointment. And please try to stay out of trouble for heaven's sake."

He signaled to the guards who were observing Patricia through the glass pane in the door. They came in and escorted Patricia out.

CHAPTER THREE

****

Patricia was in the cafeteria eating at a table all alone.

Carol Witherspoon approached her with a tray of food and asked, "Do you mind if I sit here with you?"

Patricia replied, "I don't give a shit where you sit!"

Carol looked at Patricia with animosity. Carol had always been respectful to her. Patricia had a table to herself during meals, most of the time. The other inmates generally chose to give her some space because they felt threatened by her. However, Carol thought she could get through Patricia's thick skin. Her mind-set was similar to Doctor Morgan's. So Carol did sit down at the table with a little reluctance. She had a bone to pick with Patricia and wanted to cut through the chase.

She said, "Patricia what the hell is your problem? You keep running around here like that and you are going to get beat down or taken out. These women are not going to keep taking your shit."

Patricia looked at Carol and rolled her eyes. Surely she was not directly challenging or threatening Patricia but that is how Patricia perceived it. Patricia looked at Carol like she did not know what she was talking about.

Patricia talked even with her mouth full of food and said, "Look, I just do not believe that they can help me. Shit, do you think anyone here gives a damn about what happened to us? They don't care! You see we are forgotten just like everyone else in this dump."

Carol paused a few seconds, pushed her tray of food aside and looked right at Patricia. Carol was starting to wonder if she could even get to Patricia, but she was certainly not giving up.

Patricia just shrugged her shoulders and said, "To tell the truth I just want to forget about it. It hurts so badly and I do not want to keep reliving it over and over."

Carol said, "Like I said in the session, holding the pain in and just hoping it goes away will only be detrimental to you."

Patricia finally broke down and said, "I am just confused and scared."

It was almost like Patricia was looking for someone she could confide in to tell her story to. Hearing Carol's story earlier did have a profound effect on Patricia.

"Do you think you are the only woman who has gone through this shit? Every last woman in the program has a story to tell. Some of their stories are different and some of their stories sound very much alike, but they all have terrifying stories to tell. I am sure your story is just as terrifying as the rest of the women from the sessions but it definitely needs to be told," Carol reminded Patricia.

Patricia looked doubtful and with an unbelieving expression said, "I don't know I guess so."

Carol said, "You do not have to feel ashamed of what you did. I am sure it came down to you protecting yourself and killing your husband was most likely self-defense."

Patricia bent her head down as tears formed in her eyes. Carol knew that at this point she was breaking through Patricia's thick skin. Carol handed Patricia her napkin to wipe her eyes.

"I once tried to bottle up the rage inside of me. It tore me apart from the inside out and I even thought about ending it all. I did not get any relief until I told my story in a group setting," Carol said as she started to get emotional.

Carol had told her story many times at the sessions. She had already finished the state mandated program but chose to stay in the program so she could motivate and change the lives of other victims.

Patricia paused for a second to wipe her eyes. She shook her head and tried to hold back her tears. This was not the tough image everyone in the prison came to know. Patricia turned her head away from Carol. She simply could not let Carol see the tears streaming down her face.

Patricia said, "You don't understand. It does not make me feel any better to talk about what happened. In fact, it makes me feel worse."

Patricia tried going to one of those programs when her husband started beating her. Some of the women in that program were beaten half to death and had notable bruises, cuts and scars. Just seeing them caused her to have terrible nightmares for weeks. After that, she never wanted to go into any domestic violence program. One of the Caucasian guards came up to the table and just stood there watching Patricia and Carol with a mean look for a minute.

"You two Princesses need to hurry up so the next group can come in and eat!" the guard yelled.

Carol picked up her tray and went to empty it. Patricia followed her to empty her own tray.

Carol patted Patricia on her back and said, "Girl you just need to stay strong. Just remember that all those women in the program are not only victims. They are also like your family."

CHAPTER FOUR

****

Patricia was escorted into Doctor Morgan's office by two huge black female Guards. They placed her in the seat rather harshly as she gave them a mean look. One of the Guards points at Patricia and shakes her finger to give Patricia a warning to behave. The two guards left but their presence is very much still there as they look through the door.

"Those two big bitches don't scare me! If they took these damn restraints off I would beat the shit out of both of them," Patricia said.

Doctor Morgan turned on his radio and tuned it to a soft jazz station. He turned the volume down slightly so he could communicate with Patricia but he sort of acted like he was waiting for her to settle down and tell her story. He did not want to put too much pressure on her.

"So Patricia, are you ready to do this?" Doctor Morgan asked.

She gave Doctor Morgan one of the meanest looks. She did not like the doctor's tone.

She thought there was no way this man could be getting on her case too. She did hear a little about him before he came to the facility but it was all good.

"Look Doctor Morgan, I actually changed my mind about that," Patricia said.

Doctor Morgan paused and looked at Patricia. He started tapping on the desk with his pen. He was clearly agitated.

"What do you mean you changed your mind? I had to pull a lot of strings to get you these sessions. I don't have time for games. So what is it going to be Patricia? Do you want to do this or not?" Doctor Morgan said.

Patricia said, "I meant I am ready to tell my story. That was what I changed my mind about. Just hearing the other women tell their powerful stories of abuse convinced me to tell my story. I want to be able to change the lives of other battered women. I mean I know it's the right thing to do."

"Patricia, did you know that the Hanford Women's Prison would be in the forefront of domestic violence rehabilitation? We are only the fifth prison in the whole country to receive a program that actually rehabilitates domestic violence victims on this level.

You and the other women are part of something special. So, having said that, do you want to tell your story to me now or at the group session later?"

Patricia looked up at the ceiling as if the answer was there. She looked at Doctor Morgan for several seconds and then said, "I will tell it to you first. I think it will help prepare me to tell it to the group. I guess you can call this a practice session."

"I think that would be a good idea. Would you mind me taping the session?"

She was somewhat reluctant at first because she did not understand why a tape was needed for the session. She started rocking back and forth because she was nervous.

Doctor Morgan said, "The tape is for my own personal reference and for informational purposes. Now are you comfortable? I need for you to relax and be comfortable."

"I am fine Doctor Morgan."

She said she was fine but Patricia still looked rather uncomfortable and Doctor Morgan needed her to relax.

"I will be okay. I guess I just want to get this over with," Patricia explained to Doctor Morgan.

Dr. Morgan pushed the record button on the tape recorder, spoke into the microphone and said, "I am Doctor Morgan from Hanford Women's Correctional Facility. It is the sixteenth day of November two thousand and two. The time is eleven hundred hours. I am interviewing Patricia Robinson, a victim of domestic violence, who is doing time here for killing her abusive husband."

He gave Patricia the thumbs up sign to signify the start of the session. She snatched up a few tissues to prepare herself for an emotional session. She paused briefly as she tried not to cry.

She cleared her throat and said, "Well my name is Patricia Robinson and I am serving time here for killing my abusive husband like Doctor Morgan said. I decided to tell my story in hopes it will start the healing process and I figure it might help other domestic violence victims."

Patricia wanted to take the Doctor back to the beginning where it all started. She closed her eyes and went back about two years. She flashed back to that summer and the events leading to that fatal confrontation with her husband.

CHAPTER FIVE

****

Patricia had two best friends. Yvette was an African-American woman in her twenties and Vanessa was also an African-American woman in her twenties. Both of them were very attractive. Vanessa was light-skinned with beautiful hazel eyes. She attracted plenty of brothers but she ran them away with her mouth and attitude. Yvette had light brown skin and a short, Halle Berry hairstyle. They were pretty much like sisters because they grew up together.

Yvette was the more mature one of the trio. She was happily married with a family. Vanessa was somewhat wild. She was good to hang with because you always knew she had your back. If you were friends with her and someone messed with you they would have hell to pay. She was not only the fighter of the group but she would not mind cussing you out, beating you down or even cutting you. The girls always tried to get together for lunch. They were sitting at a restaurant table outside eating lunch and talking. The weather was pretty nice as it usually was that time of the year. A small flock of pigeons landed near their table in hopes of getting a meal.

Patricia asked, "How is your husband Yvette?"

Patricia loved talking to Yvette about her marriage because it seemed to be like a big fairy tale. Yvette always seemed so happy and her relationship seemed perfect.

Yvette said, "You know girl, everything is wonderful. We are very happy and the kids are doing fine too."

Vanessa asked, "Yvette can you hang out with us today?"

"I need to get permission from my husband," Yvette replied. Vanessa and Patricia did not like when Yvette's husband stood between them having fun. It would not happen all the time but it did happen on occasions.

Patricia said, "Are you serious? You have to get permission from your man?"

Yvette said, "You two are not married so you don't know that there are rules for being married; especially if you want it to work."

"Well I am single and ready to mingle," yelled Patricia with her hands raised above her head.

Yvette said, "Patricia, while we are talking about my man I should ask you, how come you don't have a man?"

"I am okay with being single. I am just waiting for a good strong man," Patricia said as she took a sip of lemonade.

"There are plenty of strong men here," Vanessa said as she chased the pigeons away.

Patricia did not agree with Vanessa. She always had trouble finding good men and furthermore keeping them.

"I guess she needs another thug in her life. That is her idea of a strong man," Yvette said with a smile on her face.

"Patricia I think you are looking in all the wrong places. You will continue to attract the thugs if you do not change your dating habits," Vanessa said.

Vanessa looked at her watch and said, "We have about two hours before the new Tyler "P" movie. You are going Yvette, right?"

Yvette pulled out her cell phone, dialed her husband and said, "Honey I am with the girls and we wanted to go to the movies…Okay, I will be home as soon as the movie is over. It starts at two and ends at three-thirty… Okay baby, I love you too."

Vanessa and Patricia just looked at each other and shook their heads. Just like Yvette said, they did not have a clue about marriage because they had never been married.

"He said he did not have anything planned so we can hang out today," Yvette said as she put her phone away with a big smile.

CHAPTER SIX

****

Andre Robinson, a rather tall black man in his thirties, was tossing and turning in his bed. His bedroom was huge with large paintings on the wall. The room was painted all blue. He had a king-sized bed with satin sheets and pillowcases. He was having a recurring nightmare about his abusive father. The dream was when he was about twelve years old or so. He was under the kitchen table crying and trembling as he watched his father beat his mother. He darted from under the table, grabbed his father by the leg and tried to bring him down. His father flung him off his leg. Andre stood up and charged him again and his father knocked him down. He stood over Andre, waiting for him to get back up.

"You no good little bastard," yelled his father as he reached down to grab Andre.

Andre woke up and snapped up like the dead rising. He was breathing hard and he was soaked with sweat. His alarm clock was ringing loudly. He took his pillow and threw it at the clock, knocking it over. He got up and started throwing things and tearing things apart in a fit of rage. He had the rages and fits quite often. Generally, he had them after the nightmares, which were usually about two or three times a week. Sometimes he would just lie in bed for quite a while before he got up. Andre got up, reached in the nightstand and pulled out a pistol. He put one bullet it the chamber and spun the cylinder. He then put the gun to his temple and pulled the trigger. Fortunately, it was not his day to go and the gun only clicked as the cylinder turned.

"Shit shit shit!" Andre yelled out as he began to cry like a baby.

His pain from his past abuse was deep within him. There were many days, just like this one, where Andre wanted to end it all. He tossed the gun back in the nightstand, got up and started getting ready for work. He lived in a big house all by himself. He had been married before but he was a single man now.

Andre was in the computer technology field. He knew pretty much everything when it came to computers including repairing them. He was very smart and made good money. He had a lot going for him yet at this point he was once again single. He had two pictures of females on his bedroom door. They were headshots of his two ex-wives. Both photos had large red "X" marks through them. They also both had darts sticking in them as if he had been playing a game of darts with their headshots.

He grew up watching his father beat his mother and he was also a victim of his father's physical and mental abuse. The past abuse seemed to be taking a toll on Andre's relationships. He never sought help for his personal problems and chose to deal with them himself. As he got ready for work he routinely would have long one-on-one talks with himself. He even often answered himself.

Alcohol was what he used to cope with his problems and he would drink heavily at times. He could even be considered a functioning alcoholic. Andre believed that the alcohol helped him control the beast inside him. If nothing else, it helped him deal with, or at least temporarily forget about his past. It was as if he had a split personality.

At work he performed all his tasks in a timely manner and had even made employer of the year last year. Women seemed to be very much attracted to Andre because he was tall and handsome. However, he was somewhat selective. He sought women he could completely control and he had no problem finding them. He had been single for quite a while now and he was ready to start another relationship. He did not like the single life because his loneliness only exacerbated his problems.

CHAPTER SEVEN

****

Patricia was staying with her parents for a while. The economy was pretty bad and she was laid off for quite some time. She had just recently got the call to come back to work but she had already lost her home to foreclosure. Her step father, Charles, was hard-working and very strict. He was a tall, dark-skinned man in his fifties. He looked young for his age but he was not in the best shape, appearance-wise. He had short hair and a thin mustache. Patricia was like the daughter he never had. He practically raised her from when she was about six or seven. He was very protective of her, even now that she was grown. Growing up, Patricia would not dare bring a boy to the house.

She was still reluctant to let her male friends meet her stepfather. Patricia seldom heard her mother and Charles argue. Charles pretty much was the king of the castle and what he said usually went. She did remember her real father, Derrick, from her childhood.

She used to watch Derrick physically and mentally abuse her mother for years. She tried not to dwell on it too much because it gave her nightmares. Patricia's mother was single for a while after she left Derrick. After she left Derrick, she fell in love with a guy named Richard. Richard molested Patricia from the time he moved into the house. That turned out to be several years. The bastard even took her virginity. Donna actually did get engaged to Richard. Fortunately, Donna decided not to marry him. He started becoming a lot like Derrick and Donna did not want to continue raising Patricia in that environment.

Patricia never told her mother about the molestation. Her mother, Donna Robinson, was very easy-going and laid back. Donna was sort of old-fashioned. Donna was a short and light-skinned black woman. She had shoulder length, jet black hair. That was probably from the American Indian side of her. She was in her fifties, but still attractive. She grew up on a farm in the mid west and lived there a good portion of her life. Charles and Donna had been married for over twenty years and he moved her and Patricia from the country away from her family for a while. Now they were back near the city. Their home was small with a fireplace in the living room. The smell of Donna's home cooking was in the air.

They were all eating breakfast together as usual. Donna could really throw down in the kitchen. Charles always praised her cooking and went back for seconds and sometimes thirds.

"Damn this is good baby," Charles said while stuffing his mouth, licking his fingers and reading the newspaper at the same time.

"Well don't get any on the walls or the ceiling honey," Donna joked.

Charles was always running behind in the morning and Patricia was his personal time-keeper. He had to be at work by ten.

"Daddy you are going to be late again," Patricia said while pointing to the clock.

"By the way, I will be home late tonight because I need to catch up on some things at work," Charles said.

Donna said, "I will have your food in the refrigerator waiting for you just like always."

There were many times when Donna climbed in bed by herself when Charles had to work late. It was not too bad lately because Patricia was staying there now.

"I am going over to Vanessa's house right after work so I may not be here later either," Patricia said while loading another portion on her plate.

"Well, I guess I will be here by myself. Looks like it will be a Blockbuster and popcorn night," Donna said sadly.

Charles said, "Patricia, make sure you call the house, Donna's cell or my cell if you have any problems."

They all had cell phones and they had each other on speed dial. He often worried about Patricia when she stayed out late. In his mind she was still his baby girl and his job was still to protect her. Donna really did not have a problem with Patricia staying out late. Donna thought Patricia was still a virgin and would stay that way until she got married. For some reason Patricia was okay with her mother believing that. Patricia and Donna were pretty close. Donna believed Patricia was still a virgin based on one of their woman-to-woman talks. Charles was stretching and yawning like it was the end of the day. He had a full belly now and was ready to go to sleep.

"Honey, I will make your coffee strong and put it in your thermos so you can take it with you," Donna said.

Donna's coffee was so strong you could almost stand a spoon up in it. It was pure rocket fuel and it could wake the dead. She always made sure Charles took some with him to work. After all, she wanted to make sure he got through the day because he was the bread-winner.

Charles gathered his things so he could leave. He kissed Donna then Patricia and then headed out the door. Patricia needed to leave soon also but she always made the time to help her mother clean up. She felt the least she could do was to help out. She was pretty much living there rent free.

She offered to pay rent but her father would not go for it. He told Patricia she was his daughter and he would not accept any money from her. She still managed to slide some money to Donna now and then. Donna was extremely frugal and could hold money like a pit bull. That benefited all of them because Patricia and Charles were not good at saving money. Patricia gathered her things and prepared to leave for work. Donna stood between Patricia and the front door. She did that so Patricia would give her a hug and it always worked.

She acted like Patricia was a little girl and she was leaving for her first day of school. Donna really liked having Patricia there in the evenings.

She had someone to talk to and pass the time with when Charles was gone. Patricia gave Donna a long hug and headed out. Donna just went to the living room, sat on the couch, grabbed the remote and turned on the television. It was pretty much like most of her days at home alone.

CHAPTER EIGHT

****

Patricia rushed into her office cubicle because she was running a little behind. Strangely, she was good at helping Charles stay on time for work. However, that day she was late herself. She turned on her computer but it did not work. She tried everything to get it to work but she is not able to. She signaled her boss, a sort of geeky Caucasian man in his thirties, to come over and check out the computer.

"It's not working," Patricia said with a puzzled look on her face.

Her boss looked at her for a moment and said, "You won't be working here either if you come here late one more time."

He tried to get Patricia's computer working but he was unsuccessful. He picked up the phone and called for a Computer Technician. As her boss left, Patricia flipped him off behind his back. She started writing in her entries manually.

About thirty minutes later the Computer Technician, Andre Robinson, stuck his head in Patricia's cubicle. He sort of startled Patricia and she jumped.

"May I help you?" Patricia asked.

Andre held out his badge, which was hanging around his neck, and showed it to Patricia.

"I am the computer technician. I was told your computer was down," Andre said as he stepped a little further into the cubicle.

Patricia said, "Well feel free to step on in."

Patricia was clearly attracted to Andre and she just could not take her eyes off him. In his first few minutes with Patricia, he had already been undressed and done some pretty kinky things to her in her mind. Andre just stood there as if he was shy. Patricia gestured to Andre to come closer. When he did, she took his badge and looked at it more closely.

"Andre Robinson. That is a nice name. I like that," Patricia said in a flirtatious manner.

Andre knew Patricia was coming on to him but he wanted to keep it professional in the office. Actually, he was sort of feeling Patricia too. Usually, Andre did not date women he met on his job but perhaps he would make an exception this time.

"Oh I am sorry, my name is Patricia Campbell," Patricia said enthusiastically.

Patricia just stood there for a minute staring right at Andre. Andre cleared his throat to get Patricia's attention.

"Well let me get out of your way so you can do your job," Patricia said as she stepped aside. She did get his hint.

Even as she sat in her seat she just could not take her eyes off Andre. She had not seen any man come in the office that she was attracted to. Andre was definitely the exception to the rule. Patricia was usually too busy to recognize the other guys in her office or guys who came in the office. Certainly none of them made her feel this way.

"I am going to go back to the break room now so if you need anything just ask someone here in the office for it," Patricia said as she headed out of her cubicle.

"Is there some coffee back there?" Andre asked as he caught up to Patricia.

Patricia said, "Hell yeah they have coffee and it is pretty damn good too."

Surprisingly, she liked the coffee from her job better than her mother's coffee.

"I guess I could use a cup or two this morning," Andre said as he followed Patricia down the hall to the break room.

Patricia was pouring Andre's coffee but she was still staring at him. The coffee began to flow out of his cup and run down the counter.

"Whoa!" Andre yelled as he jumped back.

Patricia jumped also as she up righted the coffee pot. Andre took some paper towels and started drying up the mess.

"Sorry about that Andre," Patricia said as she grabbed some paper towels and assisted Andre.

It was certainly a good thing neither of them got burned. The only thing that was burned was Patricia's pride. She was truly embarrassed.

"I am so sorry Andre. I guess I'm a little clumsy this morning," Patricia said as she threw the used towels in the trash.

One of the nosey females of the office, Charlotte, came into the break room. Charlotte was a Caucasian female in her thirties. She dressed like she was seventy. Her fashions were definitely out of date. Her shoes looked like she got her monies worth out of them back in the seventies.

Andre and Patricia headed back to the office cubicle after Patricia signaled for them to leave the break room. Suddenly they did not need coffee anymore. Patricia's main mission was to get out of there and away from Charlotte. Andre worked on the computer for only a few minutes. He turned on the computer to make sure all the systems work properly.

He said, "Patricia your computer is as good as new," as he put his tools back in his bag.

"Wow that was fast. How long have you been a computer geek? I mean technician," Patricia asked with a childish laugh.

"About five years or so," Andre replied.

Patricia said, "I have been working here for about two years and never had the opportunity to meet you."

"That's because our contract with your company is fairly new. I think the other company went south of the border," Andre said as he looked at his watch and then the exit.

Andre needed to make his exit so he looked at his watch again and said, "Patricia I need to get going. It was certainly nice to meet you."

He reached in his pocket, gave Patricia one of his business cards and said, "You can give me a call later on if you want, but now I need to roll."

"Would I be calling for business or pleasure?" Patricia asked Andre with a seductive voice and savvy smile.

"Well feel free to call me anytime. I am single and I did not see a ring on your finger, so I assume you are not married."

Patricia had trouble believing a man who looked like Andre could really be single. She felt it was too good to be true. After all, it was not every day Patricia would meet a guy who at least seemed nice and charming. He definitely did not seem to be like the thugs she had gotten accustomed to meeting.

"If I call you I am not going to get cussed out by some crazy bitch, right?" Patricia asked.

"No, I promise you will not get cussed out by anyone. If you do it will be by me, because that is my personal cell number. I am the only one that answers it," Andre joked.

CHAPTER NINE

****

Several days later, Patricia was getting ready for a date with Andre. Her parents looked at her strangely because Patricia was quite bubbly.

"Okay Patricia, tell us what's going on," Charles said.

Patricia said, "There is nothing going on. I just happen to be in a good mood."

Donna just looked at Patricia for a few seconds and said, "Patricia Just at least tell us his name for crying out loud."

You see it was not the first time Patricia had that look about her. Donna knew that was the look of Patricia meeting someone.

Patricia finally came clean and said, "I met a guy on my job a few days ago. He just seems so nice. And he is not a thug daddy!"

Patricia would almost rather keep her relationship with Andre a secret. She knew her parents would eventually talk her into letting them meet him. She knew he would have to endure an intense evaluation and background check from Charles.

Patricia wanted to avoid some of the questions about Andre so she said. "I need to finish getting ready, so I will be back in a few."

"What time should we expect you back tonight?" Donna asked.

Patricia was not too sure what Andre had planned and could not really answer that question. She was not even sure she would be coming home that night. She knew she would never hear the end of it if she stayed out all night.

"At least tell us where he lives. He could be a damn ax murderer or serial killer for all we know. Hell, tell us something about this guy." Donna pleaded.

Patricia said, "I will try to be home by about eleven or twelve. I will write some pertinent information about Andre before I leave."

She had to tread lightly with Charles because he still was protective of her and really did not want her dating anyone. Besides, she was living in his home, so she had to walk a thin line.

She felt she should abide by some of his rules if she wanted to stay there and keep the peace. A little while later, Patricia came out of her room with one of her nicest outfits. It certainly would not be considered her Sunday best. She probably would never wear a provocative outfit like that to church. She was really looking sexy with her hair and nails nicely done. Her shoes had at least four-inch heels. They were open-toed and revealed her well manicured toes. Everything she had on was matched up real well. Her dress was form-fitting and a dark blue color. Patricia's primary mission was to thoroughly impress Andre. She knew this outfit would most likely do the job.

"Where are you two planning to go tonight?" Donna asked as she wiped down the coffee table.

Patricia looked at Donna strangely at first but then said, "I am not sure but I think we will be going to dinner. I guess he wanted to keep it a secret."

Charles gave Patricia a thorough head-to-toe evaluation. You could tell by his expression that he did not like her outfit.

He really did not need to say anything because both Donna and Patricia could read him quite well. He just went to the living room, fell in his favorite reclining seat and turned on the television. He would most likely be up until Patricia came back home. He often felt Patricia was getting back at him for being so strict on her when she was a little girl.

CHAPTER TEN

****

Patricia and Andre walked into a very nice and romantic restaurant. A Waitress, Tammy, led them to their table. The tables all had lit candles and flashing colorful lights illuminated the place. A live band played soft jazz on a stage. Tammy, a young attractive black woman in her twenties, seated Andre and Patricia and hands them both a menu.

"Hello, my name is Tammy. I will be serving you this evening. Is there anything I can get you two started on?" Tammy asked.

Patricia said, "Um I guess I will have a diet seven up."

Andre said, "I will start with a nice glass of Merlot."

After Tammy left, Patricia felt it was time to ask Andre some more personal questions. She thought this would be a good time to open Andre up a little.

"So, tell me something about yourself Andre," Patricia said while adjusting her plate and silverware.

Andre started to talk to Patricia but he was abruptly interrupted by Tammy as she asked, "Are you folks ready to order?"

Patricia glanced through the menu and said, "I will try your steak and lobster special, potato wedges and a Caesar's salad."

Andre took his time looking through the menu. He knew what he wanted already but he was really sort of checking out Tammy.

"I guess I will have the honey barbecued ribs, a baked potato and Cole slaw," Andre said as he handed Tammy his menu.

Tammy walked away after writing Patricia and Andre's orders.

"Patricia, you have not said whether you like this place or not. I went out of my way to get this place for us," Andre said in a disappointed tone.

Patricia looked around and said, "Oh I think the restaurant is beautiful and I definitely appreciate the date."

Andre just did not seem to believe Patricia. He thought she might be telling him what he wanted to hear. So he thought he would soften the mood by tricking her.

"I am glad you like this place because we are going Dutch to-night," Andre said with a very serious and convincing face.

So convincing that Patricia actually believed him. She certainly was not prepared to pay anything for this night out on the town. She was expecting Andre to be a man and handle the date.

"We're doing what?" Patricia asked.

Andre laughed out loud and said, "I was just joking. Damn, you should have seen the expression on your face. You looked like a child getting his favorite toy taken away. Shoot, I would never do that on the first date. Oh yeah, you want me to tell you something about myself. Well, I can tell you my life might be a best seller. I actually came from a broken home."

Patricia said, "Oh Andre I am so sorry for prying. My intention was not to spoil the romantic mood."

Andre said, "That's cool because I don't mind talking about my life."

Andre believed he was completely over his traumatic childhood so telling his story was somewhat therapeutic for him. He knew it was early in the relationship to tell her his story but he felt comfortable with Patricia.

Tammy came back to their table, set their food down and asked, "Is there anything else I can get you folks?"

Patricia said, "I just want a glass of water."

"I would like a refill on the Merlot," Andre said.

When Tammy left, Andre started to have second thoughts about telling his story in the restaurant. He felt perhaps it was not the right time or place for him to tell his story.

Andre put salt on his food and said, "You might be right about my story spoiling the mood. I don't think this is an appropriate place."

Patricia was disappointed because she felt he was about to open up to her. Her interest was aroused and she was ready to hear Andre's story. Tammy came back and placed some dinner rolls, water and the Merlot on the table.

"Can I get you folks anything else?" Tammy asked in a cordial manner.

Patricia was not feeling the repeated interruptions by Tammy. She thought Tammy was interrupting them on purpose. Patricia was a bit insecure. Even though Andre was not officially her man she still felt like Tammy was being disrespectful. Every time she came to their table she was smiling and checking out Andre. Patricia actually caught Andre checking Tammy out too. Tammy was very attractive, with a beautiful figure and that night she looked scantily clad. They were not at a Tooters restaurant so Patricia wondered how Tammy got away with dressing that way. She looked a lot more tempting than Patricia did that night.

"No, we are fine!" Patricia yelled.

Tammy was startled and jumped. She looked at Patricia like she was crazy and walked away rather quickly.

Andre wondered what Patricia's problem was and said, "What the hell was that all about? Why did you yell at the waitress?"

"I wanted to hear more about you. The anticipation is killing me and that heifer keeps coming over here disturbing us."

Andre decided to open up and said, "I basically grew up watching my father abuse my mother. My father later abused me too. My mother finally fled with me after she could not take it anymore. I have not seen my father in over twenty-five years."

Patricia was somewhat shocked and surprised that Andre would tell her his story. She would not be as willing to tell her story, which was very much like Andre's.

"So your mother raised you right?" Patricia asked.

Andre said, "That is correct. My mother raised me, my older brother and my younger sister. My older brother lives in Oregon and my younger sister lives in Los Angeles."

Patricia wiped her mouth with her napkin and asked, "Andre how is your mother doing?"

She was just being curious and that seemed to be an appropriate question.

Andre looked down for a second, looked at Patricia again and said, "She died a year ago from a massive heart attack."

"Oh I apologize for your loss and I hope you don't think I am prying too much."

"No I am okay. Telling my story is somewhat uplifting and empowering to me," Andre said.

Patricia sort of changed gears rather quickly and asked, "Have you ever been married?"

Andre smiled, shook his head yes and said, "Yeah I have been married twice before."

"You're only thirty-two and you have been married two times? Well what happened?" Patricia asked, once again prying.

"I guess I was not ready for marriage those two times," Andre said.

Patricia Jokingly said, "Andre, be honest; did you kill them?"

Andre laughed and said, "Believe me, they are both alive and well."

Patricia drank a little water and asked, "Andre do you have any kids?"

Andre said, "I do not have any kids so there isn't any baby mama drama going on here."

Patricia bragged to Andre and said, "I don't have any kids either. No man, no kids and no cat nor dog."

"So, tell me a little more about yourself Patricia," Andre said.

"Oh Andre maybe next time," Patricia quickly said.

"Patricia, you know you are wrong for not telling me about yourself!"

Patricia was feeling Andre but she did not feel comfortable enough to open herself up to him just yet.

She cut her steak and said, "I promise you I will tell you more about myself next time."

Andre asked, "Do you want to go downtown to that club called Club Spice? It is sort of like a thirty-plus club."

Patricia said, "It is still pretty early so what are we going to do after we eat?"

Andre said, "Let's go check out that action flick called, "A Cop's

Justice."

"Is that the one with Lucy Liu, Jet Li, Jackie Chan and several other great martial artists?" Patricia asked.

"Yeah that's the one. Now are you okay with an action flick? I mean, you are not into them chick flicks, are you?"

Patricia giggled and said, "As long as there is lots of action in the movie, I will do an action movie. The only flicks I do not like are horror movies. They give me terrible nightmares."

Andre took a quick bite out of one of his ribs and said, "I do not like the chick flicks. I'm okay with almost any other genre."

Andre looked under the table and said, "It's a good thing you wore flat shoes tonight. I love to dance and after the movie I plan to dance the night away with you. I am going to wear you out on the dance floor."

Patricia grinned and told Andre, "You are the one that is going to need medical attention not me. I am warning you because I can really get my dance on."

Andre just laughed it off and did not believe Patricia. Later that evening, Patricia and Andre were on the dance floor of Club Spice. Flashing and blinking lights illuminated the dance floor. The dance floor was pretty full of people doing the latest dances. Patricia was clearly the better dancer and appeared to be wearing Andre out. Other people who were on the dance floor gathered around Patricia and Andre. Andre, clearly out done and embarrassed, grabbed Patricia's arm and lead her back to the table. It was clear he is not a good loser. He took Patricia out to his car and they both got in.

Andre was exhausted. He rolled the car window down, put his seat in a reclining position and said, "Girl I should have known you would have all that damn energy."

"Perhaps you should have thought before you started running your mouth about what you were going to do," Patricia said.

Andre said, "It was the seven-year age difference between the two of us. If you were the same age you would have been in trouble. Shoot, I used to be a great dancer at one time."

"Whatever! I had a good time but I guess I better head back home," Patricia said.

Andre readjusted his seat and said, "Okay I will take you home. I wouldn't want your folks to send out a posse after us."

The next morning Patricia's co-worker, Charlotte, brought her a beautiful bouquet of long-stemmed red roses. There were balloons attached and they floated freely above the bouquet. Patricia pulled off the little card that was attached.

"I got a card too," Patricia said happily.

Charlotte smiled and said, "Yeah and the words are so sweet."

Patricia's expression changed real quickly to anger. She could not believe Charlotte had the audacity to read her card. She did not really like Charlotte because she was always in everyone else's business.

"How do you know what is on my card Charlotte?" Patricia asked.

Charlotte knew she was busted at that point. She stood there for a few seconds with the, "Deer in the headlights" look.

Charlotte wanted to get out of the embarrassing situation because the whole office was waiting for her to respond to Patricia.

Charlotte got up rather quickly, looked at the clock and said, "Whoa I better be getting back to work."

"Yeah bitch, you need to get a life and stop messing around with folk's shit!" Patricia said as Charlotte left.

Patricia read the card and a big smile came over her face. She smelled the beautiful roses. The balloons read, "Just thinking of you."

CHAPTER ELEVEN

****

Later that week, Patricia was at home talking on the telephone. She was on the phone for quite a while. Patricia liked to talk on the landline phone in the early evenings because her free minutes on her cell did not start until nine o' clock.

Donna asked Patricia, "Can Charles and I use the phone some times?"

Charles did not like Patricia being so involved with Andre at such an early point of their relationship.

"You are spending an awful lot of time with this guy Patricia. We hardly see you around here anymore," Charles said after Patricia hung up the phone.

Patricia said, "Andre is just such a nice guy."

Charles replied, "They all seem nice at first."

"You seemed nice at first too," Donna joked.

That was not too funny to Charles but Donna and Patricia sure got a good laugh out of it.

Later that afternoon Andre and Patricia were on a ferry. They were taking in the beautiful scenery. Andre went behind Patricia and wrapped his arms around her waist. They both peered over the ferry's security rails as they enjoyed the view. Patricia was enjoying every moment because obviously she did not get out often. The wind blew through her hair like a modeling photo shoot. For the first time in a long time Patricia felt special. Andre was truly showing his sort of suave side, and Patricia definitely loved it.

Later that night Patricia and Andre had a conversation in his car. The windows are notably steamed up. Andre started kissing Patricia rather passionately. He rubbed on her legs and as his hand crept slowly up her dress. Patricia grabbed his hand and gently placed it in his lap.

"So would you like to come over to my place for a while?" Andre asked Patricia.

Patricia said, "Andre I do not feel that going to your place is such a good idea. And I am saying that more for me. I know how I am feeling about you now."

"Girl we have been seeing each other for nearly two weeks yet you have never come by!"

"Maybe another time," Patricia said while rolling down her window for air.

Andre pretty much knew his chances were slim to get Patricia over to his place but he planned to keep trying.

"Why do you always ask me when it's late night? I don't want to be just your booty call," Patricia told Andre.

Andre just started the car and took off. He was clearly disappointed and felt somewhat rejected. However, he was still not ready to give up on Patricia so easily.

He looked over to Patricia with his little boy innocent look and asked, "You sure you don't just want to stop by for a minute?"

Patricia said, "Okay we can drive over there so I can see your place, but I will not go inside this time."

Andre knew that if she was willing to go all the way over to his house he would easily convince her to go inside.

A little while later, Patricia did make it over to Andre's place. However, they still had not made it out of the car. The two of them were making out so intensely they appeared to be wrestling. They both began to practically tear each other's clothes off.

"Andre hold on a second. Do you have one of those things?" Patricia asked while still breathing heavily.

Andre started fishing around and fumbling through his car for a condom. His pants were almost down to his thighs. He hoped he had at least one condom in there or this passionate evening would surely come to an abrupt end. He opened his junky glove compartment, moved a few things around and pulled out a whole box of condoms. Patricia was surprised that he would be so sexually prepared but she did not want to say anything that would spoil the moment.

"Okay baby, I will go inside with you. Just for a little while," Patricia said submissively.

Patricia was good and ready to have Andre right then and there. She could obviously see that Andre was ready too. Nevertheless, she did not feel like having sex in the car. She figured, why do it in the cramped car when she was sure it would be more comfortable in his bed? Besides, they were right in front of his house.

Andre was so excited he was about to leave the condoms in the car and jump out the car with his pants still down.

"Baby, you are forgetting something," Patricia reminded Andre.

Andre quickly pulled his pants up, fastened them and grabbed the condoms as they exited the car. At that point there was no doubt about what was going to take place. Patricia and Andre both knew what was getting ready to happen. Neither of them was going to stop this moment from happening.

They got to the front door, but because Andre was so excited, he fumbled with the keys for a little while. Patricia just sighed and stood there patiently with her arms crossed. Andre briefly paused, looked up at her and began to laugh. It appeared Patricia was sporting the Don King look. Her hair was all over the place.

She asked, "Why are you laughing?"

Andre refused to answer her. He may as well have pleaded the fifth. They finally did make it inside after Andre tried his fourth or fifth key. They busted through the front door and Andre led Patricia right back to his bedroom as if he was on a mission. Andre's house was fairly big for a bachelor pad. There was a long hall that leads back to the rooms. He had beautiful pictures hanging from the walls. He carried Patricia through the house and gently placed her in his king-sized bed. Andre made wild passionate love to Patricia for quite a while. They went at it two more times. Andre trembled wildly, made several faces and collapsed on top of Patricia for the third and last time. Patricia just gently laid Andre down next to her. Andre was clearly out of gas. After all, he had made love to Patricia three times straight and each time was for a long period. Andre just lies in the bed next to Patricia, knocked out and sleeping like a newborn. Patricia was obviously well satisfied. She laid there shaking uncontrollably. She fell fast asleep shortly after Andre.

The next morning Andre tossed and turned wildly as he had another one of his nightmares about his childhood. Patricia shook Andre waking him up. He jumped up and practically pushed Patricia out of the bed. He looked combative as he stood there in a fighting stance.

"Andre it's me. I think you were having a bad nightmare," She quickly reminded him.

Andre sat on the edge of the bed to get his bearings and shake out the cobwebs.

"It's okay, I deal with these damn nightmares all the time," Andre said.

Andre looked over at his alarm clock and jumped up suddenly to get ready for work. "Oh damn, I am going to be late for work," he said.

"Today is Sunday, you are off," Patricia told Andre.

Andre just shook his head and sat back down on the bed.

"Andre are you hungry?"

Andre said, "Yeah I am absolutely starving!"

"Do you want to go out to breakfast? There must be a waffle or pancake house near here," Patricia hinted as she lay back on the pillows.

Andre looked at her like she cussed at him and said, "Why go to breakfast when I can cook breakfast for us? I promise you I can make a nice breakfast."

Andre went to the closet, got a robe for Patricia and asked, "Are you okay with us taking a shower together? Hey, I am into the water conservation thing."

Patricia was not comfortable enough to let Andre see her naked in the broad day light. In fact she had not come from under the covers yet. However, she thought it was Andre's way of keeping things on a romantic level. She felt at that point it did not really matter anyway.

Patricia quickly put on the robe while she was still under the covers and said, "Sounds good to me but let me use your phone to call my folks to let them know I am okay. I forgot to plug my cell phone in last night so the battery is dead."

Andre did not like Patricia calling her folks so often when they are together. Patricia sometimes called them more than once when she and Andre were together.

"Damn girl you calling them again?" Andre asked with an attitude.

"Why do you get an attitude every time I call my parents?"

"Girl, you are spoiling the mood."

Patricia sat on the edge of the bed. She needed to talk about this with Andre.

"Well, you are not a damn sixteen year old but you are constantly calling your folks when we are out," Andre said.

"Maybe that's because my parents, especially my dad worry about me. Besides, they have not even met you but you had me out all night."

"That is bullshit because your parents do not need to know your every move!"

"Why are we even arguing about this? It is not a subject for discussion. Now can I use your phone or not?" Patricia asked.

Andre took the phone and sort of tossed it to Patricia. He was really upset at that point.

"Here is the fucking phone!" Andre said.

"What is your problem Andre?"

"Patricia you are the one with the problem!"

Patricia slammed the phone down and got up to leave. She started gathering her things and getting dressed at the same time. She was so angry she could have walked the nearly twenty miles to her parent's house. Andre just stood in front of the door to block Patricia's departure.

Patricia calmly asked Andre, "Would you just please move so I can leave?"

Patricia attempted to get by Andre unsuccessfully. When she finally nearly did get by, Andre grabbed her by her arm.

Patricia snatched her arm from Andre and yelled, "Let me go Andre!"

Andre said, "I'm sorry baby, I just had a terrible nightmare."

"Don't talk to me like that! I am not some slut from the hood," Patricia told Andre.

The mood was undoubtedly spoiled now because she was hurt.

Patricia once again started to push by Andre and said, "Just take me home Andre."

They paused momentarily as if to cool off. Andre put his arms around Patricia and pulled her close to him. Patricia tried to resist him just for a moment. She gave in and wrapped her arms around him. They sat on the bed and held each other.

Patricia still wanted some answers and said, "Gee, what was that all about? I mean last night was so beautiful and then we woke up ready to kill each other."

"I guess I am starting to fall for you. So, maybe I am a little afraid," Andre replied as he held Patricia a little closer and tighter.

Patricia was flattered but she wanted to know what he was so afraid of.

Before she could ask him he said, "Everyone I get close to either leaves me or dies."

"It is not your fault Andre. You can not change things that happened to you in the past. At some point you will have to try to get on with your life."

Andre did not like Patricia lecturing him on life so he quickly changed the subject.

"So, how about that breakfast, you still hungry?" Andre asked.

Patricia, now calm, said, "Andre I am starving and I'm about ready for that nice breakfast you promised."

Even though she really did not believe he was all that in the kitchen. She remembered how he told her he was on the dance floor. Perhaps this time he was doing the same thing. So far, she noticed when he bragged about something he usually sucked at it. That certainly held true with the sex. Andre had never bragged about how good he was in bed yet she felt thoroughly satisfied by him.

Andre fooled Patricia this time. He had a nice breakfast cooked up for her. The breakfast included an omelet, pancakes, toast, sausage, sliced melon and orange juice. Patricia was feeling real good because she found a man who knew his way around a kitchen. She felt he pretty much knew his way around a bedroom too.

As Patricia sat at the table to enjoy the meal she said, "Honey I am sort of feeling you too."

She just wanted to wait until the time was right to tell him. Since Andre expressed his feelings for her she felt the time was right.

CHAPTER TWELVE

****

Patricia, Yvette and Vanessa were at the beach on a beautiful summer day. Children ran around laughing, swimming and playing as their parents kept a watchful eye on them. The girls all had beach chairs and there was a large umbrella that shaded then from the sun.

Patricia said, "I really like Andre. He seems different from the other guys I have dated."

Vanessa and Yvette were surely not taking her seriously. They believed she was more in lust than anything else. Certainly they felt she just did not have any good loving in a while.

"Shit, you're worse than Yvette and you are not even married," Vanessa said.

Yvette adjusted the rather large beach umbrella and said, "Oh tying the knot is probably next for that girl. She practically lives with him now."

Patricia said, "No matter what happens the three of us will always be tight."

Sure it sounded pretty good because Yvette's marriage to Roger never stopped their friendship from being tight.

Vanessa asked, "Why haven't you allowed me and Yvette to meet Andre?"

Usually Patricia was so excited about having a man that she could not wait to show him off. She knew Yvette and Vanessa were brutally honest and she thought they would be critical of Andre.

Patricia rubbed some lotion on her legs and said, "I promise you two will meet Andre soon. Believe me, I think both of you will be impressed. This one definitely is not a thug."

Vanessa asked, "Patricia why does Andre call you and make you come home almost every time we're out? It's like he does not want you with us."

"It's not like that. He just likes to spend a lot of time with me," Patricia said as she tried to defend Andre's actions.

Three well-built African-American gentlemen walk up to the girls. They were in swimsuits and they stood over the girls as if they are waiting for an invitation. Sean was a tall, dark-skinned man in his early thirties. He had a bald head, goatee and was well-built. Robert was the shortest of the three. He was a light-skinned black man, about twenty-five years old. His eyes were hazel and he was also well-built. Barry was pretty close to

Sean's size, about six feet. He was a little lighter than Sean and about thirty years old. He was not as well-built as Sean and Robert.

"Hello ladies. My name is Sean and these are my two friends, Robert and Barry. How are you fine ladies doing on this beautiful day?"

Vanessa stood up, shook Sean's hand and said, "I am Vanessa and these are my two best friends Patricia and Yvette."

She held on to Sean's hand for a few more seconds as she sort of gave him her head-to-toe evaluation. Needless to say, she was notably impressed.

Robert asked, "Is it okay if we join you?"

Vanessa was quick to say, "Sure, you guys can have a seat with us if you like."

Yvette slapped Vanessa on the thigh because she felt Vanessa was being fast and acting desperate. Vanessa just held her hand up to Yvette as if to remind her that she is not married and basically could do whatever she wanted.

"I guess we should have asked if you ladies are spoken for. Not that it matters now-a-days," Sean said as he slid a little closer to Vanessa.

Yvette proudly and loudly said, "Well I am happily married and it definitely matters to me."

Barry asked, "Is anyone else either married or otherwise spoken for?"

Patricia was only able to get the words, "Well I am..." before Vanessa cut her off.

"She's spoken for too! She isn't married but she might as well be," Vanessa said.

Patricia kicked Vanessa to let her know she needed to shut up and mind her own business. Andre had followed Patricia and was watching her from the beach boardwalk. He had actually even brought some binoculars. Andre was clearly upset about Patricia's relationship with her two girlfriends. He believed they were influencing Patricia and he was somewhat jealous of their closeness.

Andre yelled out, "Those two bitches!"

There were other people near Andre when he had his outburst, including a woman and her young daughter and son. The woman stepped back, looked at Andre and walked off rather quickly with her son and daughter. Andre was so angry he was oblivious to his negative behavior. He pulled out his cell phone and dialed Patricia's number. He watched and waited as Patricia ignored her ringing cell phone. In fact, she even looked at her phone and then put it back in her bag. Andre shook his head and stormed away. He would surely have a bone to pick with Patricia when she got home.

"I guess I am going to have to straighten her ass out about them two whores!" Andre said to himself as he stormed away.

CHAPTER THIRTEEN

****

It is about six months later. Patricia is at her parent's home with Vanessa and Yvette. Patricia's parents are away on vacation. She poured some champagne into Vanessa's glass. Usually when the girls drank champagne, they were celebrating something. Therefore, Yvette and Vanessa knew something was up. Patricia leaned across the table and used her left hand to balance herself as she poured the champagne. Her very noticeable engagement ring could now be seen.

"Damn girl, what did you do to him? You must have rocked his world! I mean just look at that rock on your finger," Vanessa said.

Yvette picked up Patricia's hand to get a closer look at the ring and said, "Patricia you didn't!"

Patricia said, "Andre just proposed to me yesterday and I said hell yeah!"

Yvette and Vanessa were both baffled by this. They both looked at each other in utter disbelief.

Vanessa picked up Patricia's hand to also get a closer look at the ring and said, "Girl you have only known that boy for about three or four months."

Patricia took offence to Vanessa's statement and said, "It has been six months miss know-it-all and furthermore, my man is not a boy!"

Yvette said, "Vanessa is just tripping as usual. Her man is the one who is the boy."

Yvette did not want Vanessa being too harsh or stealing Patricia's thunder. Vanessa always spoke her mind but sometimes it was detrimental.

Yvette said, "Vanessa, none of your boyfriends have been worth a shit and they all have been like immature boys."

Patricia knew their conversation was leading to an argument. She placed a bowl of potato chips on the table and said, "Look girlfriends, I just wanted to hear some good advice about marriage. I mean, not that any of your advice will change my mind."

Vanessa said, "Well sister, I have never been married so Yvette is the one who should respond to anything dealing with marriage."

For once Patricia agreed with Vanessa. At least this time, her advice was good so she turned to hear from Yvette.

Yvette said, "Patricia there are no big secrets to a successful relationship or marriage. My marriage with Roger lasts because there is love, understanding, trust and respect."

"Uh-oh, looks like we got Doctor Ruth started," Vanessa said.

Yvette and Patricia said simultaneously, "Vanessa shut up!"

Patricia took a sip of champagne and said, "I actually think I have that type of relationship with Andre."

Vanessa, once again being negative, said, "How the hell do you know that after only six months? Girl you probably don't even know his shoe size!"

"His shoe size is ten and a half smart-ass!" Patricia blurted out.

Vanessa said, "Wow! So is the shoe size thing really true?"

Patricia grinned and said, "None of your business. It's for me to know and you to find out."

Patricia was not going to volunteer too much more information to Vanessa. She knew it would only be giving her ammunition.

Yvette grabbed a hand full of chips and asked, "Are we ever going to get a chance to meet Andre?"

Patricia did bottoms up with her champagne and said, "I promise you will get to meet him soon."

She took out a photo of Andre, showed it to Yvette and said, "Meantime, I will let you see a photo of my baby."

"This is him? Damn he is fine," Yvette said.

Vanessa snatched the picture and said, "Yeah he is fine. Does he have a brother?"

Patricia snatched the picture back and said, "Andre does have a brother but he would not want your ass. Besides, he lives way out-of-state in Oregon."

Yvette said, "Andre's brother is only a short flight from here. So you should go for it girl."

Vanessa leaned back in her seat and said, "Now you know damn well I don't do the long distance thing. And you know I do not do the friendly skies thing."

She had only flown one time in her life and vowed never to do it again. Most of Vanessa's boyfriends lived within a twenty-five to fifty mile radius of her home.

Yvette asked, "What did your mother and father say about you getting hitched?"

"They both think I lost it, but they will get to finally meet him on Friday," Patricia said.

Vanessa said, "Shit, I would love to be a fly on the wall when your parents meet Andre. Lord knows your father is going to act like a fool." Patricia knew her parents, especially her father, would never accept the fact she was grown. To them she would always be their little girl. After all, she was their only child.

Vanessa laughed and said, "Shit my parents were glad to see me get out of the house. I think they had a huge party when I left."

Patricia and Yvette thought that was funny. Actually, they could see how her parents would be happy to see her leave.

"So have you two set a date yet?" Yvette asked.

"We don't have an official date yet but I am pretty sure it will not be too far in the future," Patricia said happily.

"Well, I guess a congratulation and toast is in order," Yvette said.

As they clicked their glasses together Yvette said, "To a prosperous marriage."

"Yeah, congratulations girlfriend, now a real celebration is definitely in order. So, I just want to know where the party is going to be." Vanessa said.

She definitely would be there for any celebration or party. She never missed any parties or celebrations of any kind with the girls and was usually the life of the party.

Patricia said, "Well, I guess it looks like we will be doing Club Spice on Friday. It is going to be ladies' night and they will have plenty of strippers there. I reserved the back portion for us and our own personal male dancer. Since it is our night out I went all out and got "Big Chocolate Papa." I am sure he is going to show us what he's working with."

Patricia turned on the radio and the girls started doing their dance routines. It started looking like a party was getting ready to jump off right there at the house.

CHAPTER FOURTEEN

****

Friday finally arrived. This was the day Patricia's parents would get to meet Andre. Charles and Donna patiently awaited Andre's arrival. Charles read the newspaper and Donna prepared the meal. It was her famous spaghetti. As it got later and later Charles began to worry.

Charles looked at his watch and said, "Honey I don't think they're going to show."

Donna was not so impatient and believed they were just running late. It was not like Patricia to say she was going to do something like this and not follow through with it.

She calmed Charles down by saying, "They are probably stuck in traffic. I am sure they will be coming through the door any second now."

Almost on cue the front door opened and in came Patricia and Andre. Andre was well dressed with a pair of nice slacks and shirt. He was also well-groomed. Patricia was looking pretty sexy also. The four of them just stood there looking at each other.

Patricia finally spoke and said, "Oh I am sorry, Andre this is my mother Donna and my father Charles. Mom and dad this is Andre."

Even after Andre had been officially introduced, they still stood there staring at each other.

Donna finally broke the silence and said, "Oh excuse my manners Andre, you two come on in and have a seat. It is so nice to finally meet you. We have heard so much about you."

Andre smiled and said, "Well I hope it was all good."

Andre was very good at winning people over. He was a pretty intelligent guy and he was a very good communicator. He could be pretty funny at times when he wanted. These were some of the very characteristics that won over Patricia. Nevertheless, Patricia still felt that Andre's personality and bright smile would not win over her father.

"So you plan on marrying my daughter, right?" Charles asked with a very serious, stone-faced look.

Andre answered confidently and said, "Yes sir that is the plan."

Charles asked, "Andre how old are you?"

"I am thirty-two sir."

Charles Asked, "Andre are you ex-military?"

Andre looked at Patricia then back to her father and said, "No sir, I have never been in the military, why?"

"I was just curious because you keep on calling me sir. Feel free to call me Charles."

Andre was starting to realize Charles did not particularly like him marrying his daughter. He could tell that by the way Charles asked the questions. Andre wanted to take some of the punch out of Charles' questions and show Patricia he could stand up to her father.

"Look, I am sure you have a lot of questions for me, so feel free to ask me anything," Andre said.

Donna jumped right on in and asked, "Have you ever been married?"

She and Charles nearly fell out of their seats when Andre replied, "Yes I have been married twice before."

Charles asked, "What happened with the other two marriages?"

"Well, I guess I was not ready for marriage those times, but I am ready now."

Charles was still recovering from Andre's response to Donna's question when he asked, "So what do you do for a living?"

"I work on computers. I am a computer Technician."

Donna's eyes lit up like a child on Christmas morning. She felt Patricia had a man who was doing big things and making good money. Charles wanted to know as much about Andre as possible because Patricia always seemed to attract thugs.

"What about your family young man?" Charles asked.

Andre said, "I have an older brother in Oregon and younger sister in Southern California. I get to see them from time to time."

Charles asked "What about your parents?"

You could practically hear a pin drop. Patricia just looked at Charles and shook her head. She knew her father would eventually find a chink in Andre's armor. As Donna saw Patricia and Andre's reaction she knew something was not right with that question.

"I have not seen my father for many years. He abused my mother, my brother, my sister and me. My mother fled with us when we were all still young."

Andre paused for a few seconds and said, "My mother just died of a massive heart attack last year."

Donna quickly said, "Andre we certainly apologize for opening old wounds."

Charles did not seem to be too sorry because he was finding out what makes Andre tick. Moreover, that was the only way he could get to know him. Patricia took Andre's hand and stood up with him in preparation to leave.

"Andre we better get going. It is getting kind of late," Patricia said as she looked at her watch.

Fact is she wanted to get Andre out of there as quickly as possible. She felt she needed to rescue Andre from Charles. Donna felt she needed to make things right with Andre. She kind of felt sorry for him. She knew the way to most men's hearts is their stomach. She also had taken the time to prepare dinner for them and did not want Andre leaving without trying her cooking.

Donna stood up and said, "You all are not going to stay? I cooked some of my famous spaghetti."

Charles laughed and took a poke at Donna's famous spaghetti by saying, "Oh boy, and the old famous spaghetti! You two better get going while the getting is good."

"That's okay honey. You will be having soup and crackers tonight. Looks like you will be going on my famous quick weight loss plan," Donna said jokingly but with a serious face.

Andre shook Charles' hand and Donna hugged Andre and Patricia. Once again Charles gave Andre a stare down for a few seconds. If looks could kill Andre would have surely been a fatality. Charles grabbed hold of Andre's hand once again with a very firm grip.

"So I take it we will be seeing you again real soon," Charles said.

Andre grimaced notably and said, "Yeah I will be seeing you again real soon."

Charles did finally let Andre's hand go. Andre shook the feeling back into his hand while still grimacing. Charles was trying to give Andre a message and Andre was feeling it quite clearly. As Andre and Patricia got ready to walk out of the house, Andre stopped and turned around.

"By the way, it was nice meeting you two," Andre said as he and Patricia left.

"I can't pinpoint it but there is something funny about him," Charles said as he closed the door and locked it.

Donna believed Andre was a nice young man and said, "Oh honey you never liked any of Patricia's boyfriends!"

Charles said, "Obviously I have never been wrong because Patricia is not with any of those thugs now."

Donna headed to the kitchen and said, "Oh honey please! I am going to finish dinner. You ever think that maybe you ran some of the good ones away? Remember Jeff and Tyrone? They were not thugs."

"I am going to say it one more time. There definitely is something that is not right with Andre. Once again you will be saying I told you so." Donna was not going to listen to Charles' negative comments. Andre had answered all of his questions as well as hers. Donna was completely satisfied with Andre and felt he was good for Patricia. Surely she felt any man who could stand up to Charles' military-like interrogation was probably okay. Then again, Patricia did get Andre out of there before Charles could really lean into him.

CHAPTER FIFTEEN

****

It was now about three months from the infamous meeting. Andre, Patricia, Donna, Charles, Yvette, Vanessa and other friends and family are present. They were all gathered together to witness Patricia and Andre's wedding. This was an outdoor wedding with lots of flowers and decorations. It was a beautiful day and there were about thirty or forty guest seated on the lawn in chairs. The guests were mainly made up of Patricia's family and friends. Andre just had a couple of black male friends present. His brother and sister were not present.

Patricia and Andre looked like a fairy tale couple as they rode away in a horse-driven carriage. Donna could hardly get hold of herself and the tears continuously streamed down her face. Her little girl has grown up and is now married. Charles' expression looked very similar to the one he had when he met Andre. Even at the wedding, where he should have been happy, he appeared to be upset. At this point Charles still had not accepted Andre. He just knew Patricia could do better. Perhaps he hoped her "Mr. Right" would have been a doctor or lawyer.

Patricia was very happy. This was the day she waited for and she was glowing like a firefly the whole time. She did not shed one tear. In fact Andre was the one who became overwhelmed with emotion. He tried unsuccessfully to choke back his tears. Yvette cried like a baby the whole wedding. Maybe it was because she was married and could fully identify with the situation. Vanessa did not cry at all. She was always the toughest one in the group.

Neither Yvette nor Patricia had ever saw Vanessa cry. They had known each other for all those years yet never saw Vanessa cry. Even when she stepped on a nail that was sticking through a board she did not cry. Vanessa was only about seven when the incident happened. She just grabbed the board and pulled it, along with the nail, out of her foot. She barely grimaced. She was a regular "GI Jane."

Several weeks later, Patricia had come home from work early. She sat down on the couch to relax and turned on the television. It was the first time in a very long time since Patricia had any time off after work. She wanted to take full advantage of it. She fell asleep on the couch. Later on that evening Andre came home from work. He just stood there staring at Patricia for a little while. He slammed the door causing Patricia to jump up.

"What the hell are you doing?" Andre asked.

Patricia tried to get her bearings and said, "What do you mean? I got home early so I am relaxing."

Andre was clearly angry. He walked up and turned the television off. Once again he stopped and looked at Patricia with a scary, mean look and said, "You can relax after you fix my damn dinner!"

Patricia was in a state of shock. She could not understand why Andre was talking to her like that. Surely she was entitled to some relaxation time.

She did not want to make him any angrier but she asked, "Why are you talking to me like that?"

"If you don't get your big ass in there and cook my dinner you are going to wish you had!"

Patricia started a sentence and said, "But Andre I was going to…"

He cut her off and said, "Patricia you are my fucking wife now and as my wife you are going to do whatever I say. Now, that is just the way it is going to be."

He walked up to the couch and got right in Patricia's face. Pointing in her face he said, "I let you run your big ass mouth long enough and I put up with your little funky attitude long enough too. Now go cook my dinner before you really piss me off."

Patricia wisely went into the kitchen and did what she was told. She shakes her head and wonders if this is a preview of things to come as far as Andre is concerned. She was hoping it was just an isolated incident that stemmed from him having a terrible day at work. She had seen him mad before and they even had argued before like couples sometimes do, but never like this. Patricia felt terrible.

She tore off some paper towels to wipe her tears as she prepared the meal. Andre pretty much took Patricia's spot on the couch, grabbed the remote and started channel surfing like nothing ever happened. Later that evening Patricia actually ate dinner with Andre.

After Andre had eaten, he had several beers. Patricia saw that Andre had calmed down and relaxed.

Patricia said, "Andre I am going to Vanessa's house for a little while."

Andre just looked at Patricia with a mean look, looked at his watch and said, "Fine, but you better have your ass back here in two hours! Please don't make me have to come looking for you. I don't like that bitch anyway!"

Patricia arrived at Vanessa's house about twenty minutes later. Vanessa lived in a somewhat small apartment. It was cozy for her and she liked the tranquility of living alone. Yvette was already there and she let Patricia in. Yvette and Patricia went into the living room and had a seat on the couch. Yvette and Vanessa knew something was up because Patricia called the little meeting from her cell phone on the way there. Vanessa came into the living room shortly thereafter and had a seat.

"So what is it that you wanted to tell us?" Vanessa asked.

Patricia lowered her head sadly and said, "Andre went off on me earlier tonight."

Yvette's asked, "Did Andre hit you?"

Patricia said, "He did not hit me but I sure thought he would. For the first time I actually felt very afraid of Andre. It was like he was someone else."

Vanessa said, "Oh girl you have not even been married a full month yet! You interrupted my dinner for that?"

"Now tell us exactly what happened Patricia," Said Yvette.

Patricia said, "Well he yelled at me, threatened me and cussed me out because his dinner was not ready when he got home. I had just got off work and I was beat."

Vanessa shook her head and said, "I bet Andre is one of those men who expect you to wait on them hand and foot and hold down a full-time job too."

"Shit! I am not a damn robot. I was tired as hell myself when I got home from work," Patricia said emphatically.

Vanessa turned down the television with the remote and asked Patricia, "Girl you didn't see this coming?"

Patricia said, "I mean we had little meaningless arguments before but I never seen him act like that. I never have seen that type of rage in Andre's eyes."

Patricia apparently forgot about the first time they made love at his house. Andre was pretty mean then too.

Patricia continued and said, "He told me now that we are married things are going to change and that he is the man of the house so what he says goes."

Yvette wanted to insert her opinion as usual. She wanted to give Patricia the scoop about being married and help her through the situation.

Yvette said, "It is perfectly normal for couples to argue sometimes but they should never disrespect each other. Calling each other out of your names is also off-limits. Then there is that important ingredient called communication. I expect you to be able to talk to Andre normally just like we're talking. I want you to discuss the argument with Andre once he cools off."

Vanessa jumped up and said, "I knew that nigger was no good!"

"Vanessa! Why do you always have to say some negative bullshit?" Yvette asked.

Vanessa headed to the kitchen and said, "You two have too much drama in your lives for me!"

She just fanned them off and left the room. It was times like these that made Vanessa glad she was single. She always listened when Yvette's marriage was new and she was going through problems with her husband. Now Vanessa had to hear about Patricia's problems with her new marriage.

CHAPTER SIXTEEN

****

It is now the next evening after the incident with Andre. Patricia was preparing Andre's dinner. She was still in her work clothes. She was notably exhausted as she rushed around the kitchen to put the finishing touches on the meal. Andre walked in the door and looked around. The house was cleaned up very nicely. There were several candles lit in various parts of the house. Andre sat on the couch and turned the television on to the evening news. He never even kissed or embraced Patricia after his long hard day of work.

Patricia was attempting to set the tone to use one of Yvette's main relationship ingredients. She planned to simply try to communicate with Andre. She hoped he was in a better mood. She tried to have everything done right for him so he would not have a reason to become upset with her.

Patricia wiped the sweat off her forehead and said, "Hello honey, dinner is ready. How was your day?"

Andre gestured to Patricia and said, "Bring my food in here."

Patricia brought Andre's food to him on a tray. She then sat next to him and asked, "Are you sure you want to eat in the living room? I have the dining room set up for the two of us."

She had worked way too hard setting up the occasion and wanted things to go as planned. Andre started gulping down his food like a wild animal and ignored Patricia. In fact, he turned up the television a little louder. Patricia stares at him for a while anticipating his answer. This surely could not be what Yvette meant about communication.

"I am fine in here," Andre said with his mouth full of food.

"Andre I wanted to talk to you. Baby can you at least turn the television down?"

Andre turned the television down slightly.

She said, "I really wanted the two of us to eat in the dining room together."

She did not feel comfortable trying to talk to Andre with the television on. Andre still had the television quite loud.

"What do you want to talk about? Can't you see I just got home and I am not in a mood to talk?" Andre asked with a frustrated tone.

Patricia started to get a little nervous. Andre did not seem to be as cool as she had hoped. Even though she was nervous and somewhat scared, she was determined to talk to Andre on this night.

"Honey I just wanted to talk with you about the argument we had last night," Patricia said with a very soft, convincing voice.

"Well talk!" Andre shouted.

"Andre I felt the way you spoke to me last night was wrong."

She really hoped he would apologize so the two of them could get past the whole ordeal.

Andre went off on Patricia and said, "Is that really how you feel? I think you are just listening to your bitch ass girlfriends and your damn parents."

Patricia got upset and said, "Please do not talk about my family or my two best friends."

Strangely enough, he could call Patricia out of her name all he wanted but not her family or friends. She would not tolerate that.

"Will you please just shut the fuck up before you spoil my appetite!" Andre shouted.

The previous evening was fresh on Patricia's mind and she felt this discussion was heading in that direction like an out of control locomotive. She was somewhat speechless for a few minutes and had no idea what to say next.

"But honey, I thought we could discuss what happened last night over dinner," Patricia said with a soft voice.

"There is nothing to discuss! You will have my dinner ready for me when I come home every damn night. No ifs ands or buts! In fact, I want you to put in your two-week notice to your job tomorrow," Andre said as he bites off a huge chunk of chicken leg like a caveman.

"Patricia I make enough money so you do not need to work."

"Baby I would not feel right about that. I like my job. Besides, two salaries will always be better than one."

Andre was clearly getting more and more annoyed with Patricia. Patricia looked at Andre like she was going to talk again but Andre put up the "talk to the hand" sign to shut Patricia up. He was really warning her that he had heard enough and she had better stop while she was ahead.

Patricia started talking anyway and said, "Andre I just don't think that you're being fair. I should be able to have a say in a decision like this."

Andre threw his plate of food towards her and said, "You satisfied? You spoiled my whole damn evening and managed to piss me off all in a matter of minutes. Now, clean that shit up and get me another plate of food!"

Patricia just stood there for a minute, basically in shock. It was as if she was frozen.

Andre pointed towards the kitchen and said, "Move your big ass!"

Patricia brought Andre out another plate of food. She went back in the kitchen and returns with a rag, broom and dustpan to clean up Andre's mess.

"You better wipe that look off your ugly face girl."

"Andre I should not have to put up with this kind of treatment. I have done nothing wrong."

"Patricia shut up because I am already pissed off."

Patricia attempted to storm away with an attitude. She had put up with all she could and did not plan on taking any more.

"Fine!" Patricia shouted.

Andre jumped up off the couch, grabbed Patricia by the arm and said "I told you I am not going to put up with your crap anymore!"

"Andre you are hurting me," Patricia yelled.

Andre slapped Patricia across the face and said, "See what you made me do? I told you to shut up."

Patricia sat down on the couch and began to cry as she held her eye. With that slap Andre marked the beginning of the physical abuse. Oh he had grabbed her by the arm before but he had never struck her. Andre watched her for a minute and then shook his head. He was feeling somewhat remorseful at that point. He sighed and sat next to Patricia to console her.

He rubbed her back for a minute and said, "I am sorry baby. I didn't mean for that to happen. I just had a bad day at work today. My boss was on my ass all day."

Patricia said, "Baby what is happening to us? I feel like we're growing apart and that all we do is fight now."

Andre started running his hand through Patricia's head and said, "Nothing is the matter with us or the relationship. We still love each other, right?"

"Andre you just struck me."

"Baby, I am sorry and I promise you it will never happen again. Look baby, you know I love you. You know I would never do anything to intentionally hurt you and you know that was not me a few minutes ago."

Patricia replied, "I am willing to let it go as long as it will not happen again. Honey we need to try to get along better."

Andre hugged Patricia and said, "Everything is going to be all right."

Andre moved Patricia's hand from her face so he could view the damage he caused. Actually he gave her a black eye. He went into the kitchen and came back with an ice pack and handed it to Patricia.

Andre tried to downplay Patricia's bruise by saying, "Patricia your eye is not too bad. I assure you the whole incident was just a terrible mistake that will never happen again. I still insist you give notice at your job."

Patricia reluctantly said, "Okay Andre, I will put in my two-week notice tomorrow."

At this point she would do anything for Andre to keep the peace.

CHAPTER SEVENTEEN

****

Yvette and Vanessa were over at Patricia's house this time. Patricia wanted Andre to meet Yvette and Vanessa so he would realize they were good people. Perhaps he would see why they are her best friends. Yvette and Patricia played Scrabble while Patricia quickly prepared Andre's food. She knows Andre will be home soon but she takes the opportunity to sit down with the girls for a while.

She was wearing shades in the house, which Yvette and Vanessa thought was strange. They quickly figured out what was going on but they wanted to wait for Patricia to talk about it. Patricia finally did take her glasses off, revealing her black eye.

Yvette could not sit there quietly anymore. She said, "Girl what happened to your eye?"

Patricia paused for a second to make something up. She said, "I fell down the porch stairs."

Vanessa asked, "How the hell did you manage to fall on your face?"

Patricia became annoyed and said, "I just happened to trip so can we move on to another topic?"

Yvette said, "No way girl! We are not going to go to another topic."

She and Vanessa knew what the deal was but they wanted Patricia to be honest with them and tell them what happened.

Yvette said, "Patricia we all go back a long way so you know Vanessa and I were not born yesterday."

"Andre did that didn't he?" Vanessa asked.

Patricia once again paused and said, "Yeah he got a little upset and hit me. Now you know, so are you two satisfied?"

Vanessa spoke her mind just like always and said, "You need to give his ass the Al Green treatment!"

Yvette asked, "Vanessa what the hell are you talking about?"

Vanessa quickly explained and said, "She needs to throw some hot grits on him. That's what I would do."

Yvette said, "Vanessa please shut up! So, Patricia what are you going to do next? I mean, my main concern is that I think Andre crossed the line once he struck you."

"Yeah, I know but he apologized to me and promised it would never happen again. I guess I want to give him another chance."

Vanessa said, "They all say they will never hit you again or they simply apologize each time they hit you. Patricia, if he hits you once he will most likely hit you again."

Patricia said, "I was concerned too at first, but I still believe Andre truly loves me. He just has a bad temper."

Vanessa was just being nosey as she asked Patricia, "Have you told your folks about this latest incident?"

Patricia said, "No because I did not want to upset them for nothing."

She knew they would be upset with Andre. She knew her father would definitely go after Andre if he knew what was going on.

"Patricia upset them for nothing? You call getting struck by your husband nothing?" Yvette said as she got up and paced the floor.

Patricia replied, "Yvette it was just a little fight. I think Andre and me will be fine. Shit, you don't know what he has been through."

Andre had snuck in without the girls hearing him. He had been standing at the doorway listening for a while.

Not noticing Andre, Vanessa said, "If you ask me I think he is crazy. From what you said about his childhood, he fits the profile of boys that grow up to be men who rape, kill, abuse and goodness knows what else. His crazy ass probably does need some help."

Vanessa noticed Patricia and Yvette looking over towards the door with a petrified look on their faces. Vanessa turned around and saw Andre standing there with his arms on his hips. He appeared to be drunk already.

"Patricia, I want those two bitches out of here!" Andre said with slurred speech.

Vanessa jumped out of her seat and said, "Just who the hell are you calling a bitch?"

Patricia said, "Vanessa and Yvette I just need you two to leave. Please."

She went up to Vanessa to restrain her from Andre. She then escorted Vanessa and Yvette to the door right past Andre. Vanessa took a lunge towards Andre but Yvette and Patricia restrained her.

"You need to teach your man some respect," Vanessa said.

Andre never flinched or budged. He acted like he knew or at least assumed Vanessa was not going to attack him. He never feared a woman in his life anyway.

Yvette pulled Vanessa by the arm and asked, "Patricia are you going to be all right?"

Andre said, "She is going to be just fine as soon as you two get the hell out of my house!"

Vanessa stopped one more time, turned around and said, "If you need anything girl just give us a call. We will be over here in no time. I am about two seconds off his ass now!"

Vanessa and Yvette do finally leave as Andre slams the door behind them. He looks at Patricia with disdain and says, "I thought I told you I don't want you with those two bitches."

Patricia replied, "Andre you said you do not like them but you never told me I could not be friends with them or hang with them."

Andre did not like Patricia correcting him so he gave her a dirty look and said, "Well now I am telling you. I do not want you with them anymore!"

Patricia said, "Baby, Yvette and Patricia are like my two sisters. We grew up together, and we have always been inseparable."

She felt the need to convince Andre to change his mind. She knew she had to tread lightly because Andre was already pretty pissed.

Andre said, "Yeah right. They pretend to be your friends so they can know all your damn business. Shit, they know more about you and me than we do."

Patricia told Andre, "We do discuss various issues and problems together but that is what girlfriends do."

Andre wanted to isolate Patricia from her friends and he felt this would be a good reason and a good opportunity.

He said, "What happens in this house should stay in this house. It is nobody else's business. Not even your parent's."

Patricia said, "Okay baby, I will not discuss our problems with Yvette and Vanessa."

Andre still was not completely satisfied and said, "You need to include your nosey ass parents in that deal too."

Patricia did not like Andre's request in regards to her best friends and she disliked this one a lot more. Surely Andre could not be serious about what he was saying. She was very tight with her parents, especially her father. She could even discuss things with him that most girls would approach their mothers to talk about.

"But you don't expect me too…" Patricia said.

Andre once again cut her off and said, "I expect you to do whatever I tell you to do. I told you I am your husband now not your damn boyfriend. There is a big difference. Your ass belongs to me now."

Andre walked up to Patricia, pushed her so hard she nearly fell backwards and asked, "You have anything else smart to say you fat bitch?"

Patricia was nearly at a lost for words but did say, "You promised not to treat me like this anymore."

This angered Andre even more. He grabbed Patricia by her arm, pushed her back on the couch and said, "Just sit your big ugly ass down and shut up!"

Patricia got up to storm away once again. She was heading to the door with plans of going to her parent's house or one of her girlfriends' houses. She actually had some of her clothes and toiletries at each of the houses, so she was prepared to stay away from Andre if she had to. Just as she made it to the door and opened it, Andre caught up to her.

He grabbed her by her arm, spun her around with force and said, "I am tired of you running to your damn parent's house all the time. You see they spoil you and let you have your way but I am not going that route with you! You are going to do what I tell you to or I am going to make you pay."

Patricia makes a futile attempt to get free of Andre's grasp but she only made him madder. He grabbed her and started shaking her violently like a rag doll. He stopped shaking her momentarily, only to catch his breath.

"Andre I don't deserve this," Patricia said as she began to weep.

Andre shoved Patricia into the wall so hard he left her imprint in the wall.

He said, "Oh you deserve every bit of this bitch!"

He threw Patricia on the couch and began to punch her about her head and face. Patricia covered her head and face as best she could, hoping Andre would run out of gas or just stop beating her. He did run out of gas after a while. He walked away and went to bed as if nothing even happened.

CHAPTER EIGHTEEN

****

Later that night, Patricia did manage to make it over to Vanessa's house. Vanessa had out a first aid kit with bandages and some ice packs. Patricia looked like she had gone several rounds with Mike Tyson. However, she did not go to the hospital. Yvette has also come over to Vanessa's house to give Patricia support. Patricia still attempts to explain it all away.

She started out by saying, "Andre just needs some help."

Some of what she says can't be understood. It is as if she is muttering words to herself. She appears to be in shock.

Yvette said, "Patricia don't be so naïve. I mean Andre really beat you up bad this time."

Vanessa applied an ice pack to Patricia's head and then wrapped a bandage loosely around her head to hold the ice in place.

Vanessa said, "Now I am not a doctor. I only know basic first aid and CPR. Patricia you sure you don't want to go to the hospital?"

Patricia said, barely audibly, "No I am fine."

Yvette and Vanessa wanted to call the police so they could lock Andre up, at least for a while. Perhaps Patricia could then have the opportunity to get a restraining order and some help.

Yvette said, "Patricia would you at least tell your parents?"

Even though she knew she and Vanessa had already told her parents.

Patricia said, "No way and you two better not either."

Vanessa asked Patricia, "What are you going to do now?"

Even Patricia realized at that point something needed to be done. She just did not know what to do or where to go. Yvette and Vanessa could only go so far with Patricia and they were quite limited in what they could do to help her. The decision to take action was strictly in Patricia's hands.

Vanessa said, "If you want I can get some guys who will be more than happy to tighten his ass up for you. You just give me the word girl."

Patricia quickly declined Vanessa's offer and said, "I do not want anyone else getting involved or getting into trouble."

Vanessa just shook her head and said, "If you keep on letting him beat on you like this you are the one who is going to need help." Patricia's cell phone rang and it was Donna.

Patricia shook her fist at Yvette and Vanessa. She knew they had told her parents.

She said to Donna, "No mom we just got in a little fight... No I am okay... No I do not want you and daddy coming by... Okay I will come by... Okay mom... I love you too... Good bye"

After she finishes her conversation with Donna, she slams her flip phone shut and just gives Yvette and Vanessa a mean look.

Patricia asked, "Now why would you two tell my parents about what happened to me?"

"We both thought it was best," answered Yvette.

Patricia knew her two best friends were doing what was right but for some reason she still felt annoyed. To her it was the principal of it that counted.

She said, "I would expect Vanessa to do something like that but not you Yvette. Thanks a lot! Now I need to go home and explain all this shit to my parents. My father is going to absolutely go "Rambo" about this."

Patricia was really upset with her situation but she was taking her frustrations out on her two best friends.

Vanessa said, "Oh girl your parents would have found out about the abuse eventually one way or the other. You can't keep thinking your make-up will hide the problem from everyone. It goes a lot deeper than that."

Right at that moment, Patricia went into her bag and retrieved a mirror and some make-up. She completely ignored what Vanessa said. She proceeded to put the make-up on rather heavily, especially around her bruises. She did not want her parents seeing her in that condition.

Vanessa said, "Girl why are you tripping about us trying to help you? We did it so you can get some help. You won't listen to us so we thought maybe your parents would have a better shot at convincing you."

Patricia got up to leave but stopped, turned around and said, "Look I am leaving. I will holler at you two another time. Bottom line is I thought I could trust you two and you both let me down."

Patricia left and Yvette and Vanessa looked at each other and almost simultaneously shook their heads. Vanessa said, "I guess we pissed her off."

Yvette said, "That is okay, she will get over it. I still say we did the right thing. She is probably going to thank us later on."

Later that evening Patricia did drive over to her parent's house. She stayed outside in her car for about two hours trying to get up enough nerve to go inside. She just could not face them that night. She had cried much of her make-up away. She flipped down the sun visor and turned on the light to the vanity mirror. She stared at her face in the mirror for several minutes.

She drove back to her house as she continued to cry like a baby. Her cell phone rang repeatedly but she did not bother to answer it. She knew it was her parents. She was obviously in no mood to explain her situation. She wanted to at least wait until the bruises and swelling in her face went down. She was hoping her father did not show up at her house.

She would never put it passed him. If he did, she was planning to not open the door. She did not believe that Andre would be bold enough to answer the door if Charles came over either. She snuck into the house knowing Andre was most likely sleeping. He was passed out on the couch so fortunately, she was able to escape his wrath that night.

CHAPTER NINETEEN

****

Andre came home from work and did his usual routine. He sat on the couch and grabbed the remote. Patricia had cleaned the house from top to bottom and the dinner was cooked. Patricia was no longer working at her job. She had completely quit and was allowing Andre to be the breadwinner as he requested.

Patricia does get to see her friends from time to time. Sometimes she avoids confrontations with Andre by going to Vanessa's or Yvette's house. There are sometimes a string of several days where Andre does not abuse or bother Patricia. In fact, there are times when he actually treats Patricia like a woman.

Patricia still had to wonder whether she would be with Dr. Jekyll or Mr. Hyde. She did not know what to expect from Andre from day-to-day. As of that night, Andre had not beaten or verbally abused Patricia for quite a while.

Patricia even had time to heal a bit. Therefore, she did finally get to see her parents. In fact, she was able to explain her problems with Andre away. Unfortunately, this was going to be one of those bad nights. Andre had started drinking. Actually, he had started drinking more heavily. The refrigerator was filled with beer, and the liquor cabinet had several bottles of liquor. Patricia could not say anything to him about it for several reasons. One he would surely attack her, two he was the one working and finally it was his money.

"Bring me a beer!" Andre yelled to Patricia.

Patricia brought Andre out a beer. Andre opened up the beer and gulped it down like a dehydrated man drinking water in the hot desert sun.

"Bring me another one!" Andre shouted.

Patricia stood there for a few seconds. She pretty much knew what his heavy drinking would lead to. She hoped he would just pass out for the night like he often did when he drank.

"Andre, you have not eaten dinner yet, are you sure you want another beer?"

"Bring me a beer!" Andre demanded.

Patricia is startled and quickly goes to the kitchen and comes back with a nice cold beer for Andre. At that point she began to sort of walk on eggshells. She was starting to learn what buttons set Andre off. Sometimes this helped and other times it did not. There were times when no matter what she said or did she got either verbally or physically abused. Patricia had not had consensual sex with Andre since they were married. She struggled to find an emotional and physical connection with Andre that did not involve the abuse. That did not stop Andre from forcing himself on her on occasions. Andre managed to polish off a whole six-pack in less than a half hour and was definitely feeling the effects.

"Come here," Andre said as he took his last gulp of his sixth beer.

Patricia slowly and reluctantly approached Andre. She thought he was going to attack her. When she got close enough, Andre grabbed her by her arm and pulled her down on his lap. As she sat there in his lap, he began to grope her breasts and body. Patricia was not feeling too sexy and became somewhat resistant towards Andre's advances. Andre began to get a little more aggressive so Patricia felt she better not resist.

"What the hell is wrong with you? You seeing another nigger, aren't you?" Andre asked.

Patricia was quite shocked at such an accusation and said, "Baby, I would never cheat on you. I am just not feeling well now."

Andre threw Patricia on the couch and said, "You been messing around with them two whores you call your friends, so there isn't any telling who you been doing!"

Patricia struggled with Andre at first but then just lays there motionless. Andre starts tearing off Patricia's blouse. He then starts slapping her as he struggles to open her pants. Patricia covers her face as best she can as Andre tugs on her pants. He pulls her pants down nearly to her ankles.

Patricia quickly slides her panties down and says, "Andre you don't have to hurt me anymore. I will make love to you."

Andre slaps her once more and says, "Shut up! I am going to treat you like the whore you are!"

Andre rapes Patricia violently. You can see the ferocity in his face. Patricia just lies there motionless and allows Andre to have his way. She knew that fighting Andre would be bad for her. Tears begin to stream down her face and blood flowed from her nose. Andre just got up, pulled his pants up and walked away when he was finished. Patricia rolled over on her side and got into the fetal position. She began to cry out loudly as she rocked back and forth.

CHAPTER TWENTY

****

Yvette and Vanessa had managed to get Patricia to a Battered Women's Shelter. They take her to the Program Coordinator, Gina Perkins' office. Gina is a rather tall African-American female, about thirty-five years old.

Gina said, "Come on in girls. I am Gina Perkins and I am the Program Coordinator here. I take it you are Patricia, right?"

Patricia was really not feeling this place. She replied to Gina sarcastically and said, "Lucky guess or did the bruises give me away?"

Vanessa jumped right in and says, "Yeah, she is Patricia, this is Yvette and my name is Vanessa. We are Patricia's two best friends. We are the ones who contacted your shelter."

Gina said, "You two are welcomed to come by during visiting hours. Trust me, both of you did the right thing by bringing Patricia here."

Patricia embraced Yvette and Vanessa for a sort of group hug.

"You two need to keep them cell phones on. I don't know if I am going to stay here. I am just not feeling it," Patricia said as Vanessa and Yvette walked away.

Yvette and Vanessa paid no attention to Patricia's statement as they continued walking away. They believed she was not talking rationally due to the abuse and was probably still in shock.

Gina said, "Patricia you have two great friends."

Patricia just nodded her head yes in agreement. Gina felt she needed to ease Patricia's anxiety.

Gina said, "Well I guess we can start with a tour of our facility. Maybe we can meet some of the girls. Now our most important rule is that you have no contact with your husband or partner while you are here. That is for obvious safety reasons."

A young woman, whose name is Michelle, walked down the hall of the facility. Michelle is a Caucasian female, about twenty-five years old. The bruises and black and blue marks on her face are quite notable. Michelle appears to have been battered violently.

Gina stops Michelle before she passes by and says, "Michelle, how are you doing? Michelle this is Patricia, Patricia this is Michelle."

Michelle is somewhat embarrassed because of her appearance. She shakes Patricia's hand while looking down towards the ground. She never really makes eye contact with Patricia or Gina. Michelle continued down the hallway very slowly and zombie-like. Patricia and Gina continue through the facility.

Patricia asked, "Is that how the women here look?"

"Some of them look like that and some look even worse, why?"

"Well, I mean she was in pretty bad shape," replied Patricia.

She was actually in considerably worse shape than Patricia, but only because Michelle had just arrived there today after her beating occurred.

Gina said, "Oh some of our girls are in pretty bad shape. That is why we have a great nursing staff here as well as a great counseling staff. Sometimes the internal or emotional wounds are far worse than the physical wounds we actually see. It is real important for us to help heal you from the inside out."

Patricia took a deep breath, shook her head and said, "Ms. Perkins I don't think I belong here."

Gina was starting to get a little nervous at that point. Patricia had looked her right in the eyes and said those words. Gina felt she was going to lose Patricia from the shelter. Gina knew she needed to convince Patricia to stay.

Gina asked, "Am I missing something? I mean your husband does abuse you right?"

"Yeah but it looks like her husband tried to kill her," Patricia replied.

Gina could see that Patricia obviously did not know how the domestic violence usually goes. She wanted to make it very clear to Patricia.

Gina put her hand on Patricia's shoulder and said, "Just because your husband has not beaten you up that bad yet does not mean he won't. In most cases the abuse gets progressively worse. Sometimes the woman even becomes a fatality."

"Oh please Gina! I do not believe Andre would go that far. He just needs to get some help for his emotional problems. He has been through hell but he has never received any help."

"Honey they all need help in some way. Some are too far gone for help. Patricia, please don't be naïve. The cemeteries are full of women who thought their man would never kill them. Young lady, do you realize that every fifteen seconds in this country an incident of domestic violence occurs?"

"Look Ms. Perkins, I appreciate all your concern but as I said, I don't feel I belong here. I think that maybe I would be taking a bed from someone who really needs help."

"Patricia I can not force you to stay. In order for you to get help you have to recognize the fact you need help."

Patricia put out her hand and shook Gina's hand.

"Thanks Gina for your time and I appreciate what you're trying to do for me and the other women."

Gina holds Patricia's hand for a few seconds. She then reaches in her pocket with her free hand and gives Patricia a business card and a brochure of the facility.

Gina said, "The National Domestic Violence hotline is on the brochure. You should get to know the number by heart."

"Oh I know it quite well Ms. Perkins. It's 1-800-799-SAFE."

Patricia took out her cell phone and dialed Vanessa's number.

"Girl I need you to pick me up…This place is not where I need to be…Shit, just forget about it! I will take a damn cab!" Patricia yelled as she slammed her flip phone closed.

Gina can clearly see what is happening to Patricia. She feels Patricia is experiencing psychological stress and anxiety from the abuse.

She said, "Patricia are you sure you don't want to stay?"

"No thanks Ms. Perkins. I think I will be okay. Could you call me a cab?"

Gina said, "Sure, I will call you a cab. You can wait for it in my office if you want."

She took out a pen and wrote her personal cell number on the back of the card and said, "Feel free to call me if you need to, but of course if you have an emergency, don't hesitate to call nine-one-one. Now I can't promise you there will be space available for you later. Unfortunately, there is never a shortage of battered women in this community, just a shortage of shelters and facilities to house them. Many women use our facilities as a safe haven. You are welcome to use any of our resource centers or facilities at any time at no charge to you. Would you at least take a look at the facility with no obligations or strings attached?"

Patricia looked around a little more and then said, "Gina I will be fine. I will wait outside for the cab."

Patricia turned around and walked down the hall with her luggage. Gina could only watch helplessly and hope Patricia did not become a statistic or much worse a victim.

CHAPTER TWENTY-ONE

****

Patricia has made it back home. Andre has gone all out to welcome Patricia back home. He has cooked a full coarse meal with candle light provided, balloons and a, "Welcome home Patricia" banner. The smooth sounds of Luther can be heard playing in the background.

Patricia was sitting at the table which was neatly made with a beautiful red tablecloth. Andre walked over, poured Patricia some Champagne. He bends down and gives Patricia a very warm kiss on the lips.

Andre said, "Baby I am so glad you came back home to me. I really missed you. I thought I had lost you forever. You know I love you, right?"

Patricia nodded her head yes, but with notable uncertainty.

Andre pulled up a chair, sat right next to Patricia and said, "I just wanted to say I am sorry for the way I treated you and I wanted to make a solemn promise that I will never hurt you again."

Andre left and came back with a bouquet of roses in a vase of water. Andre placed the roses right in front of Patricia.

Patricia took the little card off the roses and read it aloud saying, "I love you now and forever. You will always be special to me, with love always, Andre Robinson."

Her words came out sort of distorted because her lips were still pretty swollen from her previous encounter with Andre. The tears began to flow down Patricia's face.

She said, "Andre that is so sweet."

"Hold on baby I have something else for you," Andre said as he ran back into the bedroom.

He came back with a small box. He opened the box and presents Patricia with a beautiful gold necklace.

"Honey, I really hope you like this," he said as he put it around her neck.

"Baby I absolutely love it. It is so beautiful."

Patricia jumped up, hugged Andre and said, "Thank you so much baby. I love you too."

"I planned to wait until dinner was over to give you the gift but I just could not wait. Now baby, can you find it in your heart to forgive me?"

Patricia asked, "Do you promise you won't hurt me anymore?"

Andre said, "I will never hurt you again. That is my promise to you."

Patricia asked, "Would you go to marriage counseling with me or maybe see a counselor to help with your anger and nightmares?"

Patricia really did not feel it was an appropriate time to ask Andre that question. Nevertheless, it was too late and she just hoped it did not spoil the evening or set off Andre.

Andre did not like Patricia asking him that question and replied, "I don't need any damn counseling! You think I am loco or something, right?"

Patricia slowly slid backwards in her chair. She was afraid to reply to Andre or say anything else. She thought that maybe she would be better off and safer if she did not say anything.

However, she did say, "No baby I don't think you are loco. I just thought you might be able to get some help for your nightmares."

At this point she began to tremble with fear. She saw that look in Andre's eyes and it was not a pretty sight for her.

Andre said, "I been dealing with my nightmares for years. They don't even bother me anymore. We do not need a marriage counselor either. Our marriage is fine!"

Patricia wanted to calm things down. She said, "Andre let's not spoil the evening. I am sorry I brought it up. Let's just forget about it."

Andre thought about it for a few seconds and pretty much agreed to let it go but he was still clearly agitated.

Patricia wanted to make sure she got the subject off Andre's mind so she changed the subject by asking Andre, "So honey, what did you cook tonight? It sure smells good."

"I made some baked chicken, corn, rice and some dinner rolls."

"Yummy! Well let's dig in before I starve to death," Patricia said.

Andre brought the food in and set it on the table. As Andre sat down, Patricia reached over and held his hand.

She bowed her and said, "Thank you Lord for this food, which we are about to receive, for the nourishment of our bodies, for Christ's sake, amen."

They both dug in. Patricia had a wonderful evening that night. She had almost managed to spoil a perfect evening. It was by far one of her best evenings with Andre to date.

CHAPTER TWENTY-TWO

Patricia was at her parent's home about four weeks later. Things continue to get worse for Patricia the more she stays with Andre. She has once again sought shelter at her parent's house, waiting for Andre to sober up and calm down. Yvette and Vanessa are also there.

Patricia has fresh bruises to go over the older, healing bruises. She even has stitches over her right eye. Donna left the living room and came back with a hand mirror.

Donna held the mirror right in front of Patricia and said, "Patricia just look at your face. Honey this is not love."

Patricia quickly turned away as if she had seen a ghost.

"No, I want you to take a good long hard look at your face! Don't turn away, I want you to see this," Donna said.
Charles got out of his seat and was pacing back and forth like a ferocious caged lion.

He is clearly livid as he says, "Patricia this is a vicious cycle. He beats on you, you come stay with us or your friends for a short period and then you go right back to him. What could you possibly see in him at this point? You know he is not going to change."

Patricia emphatically said, "I still love him and I am not ready to throw the towel in on my marriage just yet. You don't know Andre like I do."

"Patricia this guy is no good for you and I think you know it. He has already been through two wives, most likely because he is an abuser. Now he is trying to make you the third abused ex-wife," Charles said.

Vanessa was sitting on the couch right next to Patricia. She wanted to make sure Patricia heard what she had to say. She got Patricia's attention by looking her right in the face and saying, "How long are you going to let this go on? Shoot, the police and Paramedics come to your house so often they are talking about making it one of their substations."

Yvette and Patricia's parents did not like that statement and didn't find any humor in it. Even though Vanessa was acting very serious, it seemed she was trying to slide in a little of her comical twist, as she often did. Needless to say her timing was definitely wrong.

Yvette said, "You still don't think you need to get some help or go to a shelter? I am sure you are starting to look just like some of those women you saw. Remember the ones you said really needed help?"

Vanessa jumped up and said, "I think he needs an attitude adjust-ment. I told you I know a few friends who would take care of his ass! No questions asked."

Charles jumped up and grabbed his, "Walking Tall" stick and headed to the door. Vanessa follows right behind him as if she wants a piece of the action too.

Charles said, "Shit I can take care of his ass myself!"

Donna caught up to Charles and snatched the stick away from him. She asked Charles, "Baby have you lost your mind?"

Charles said, "I just wanted to talk to Andre."

Charles headed back to his seat and said, "What the hell am I supposed to do? That son-of-a-bitch is hurting Patricia!"

Vanessa quickly returned to her seat, sat down and acted like she was not a part of the outburst.

"Honey I guess you have lost your mind. You are not acting any better than him now," Donna said as she sat down next to Charles with the stick still in her hand.

"Look, I just want to go face-to-face and toe-to-toe with him and find out what his problem is," Charles said.

Donna said, "If you go out there with the stick you would be doing the wrong thing and I think you know it."

"Well I am tired of sitting around and doing nothing." Charles said.

Donna said, "Believe me Charles, you are not the only one who feels like that. We all would like to go down there and have a piece of Andre. I can't let you do this. What good would it do? You would be in jail for assaulting him and he would still be beating Patricia."

Patricia had listened long enough and finally said, "Look I don't want any of you to get involved. He knows you all are trying to get me away from him and believe me he is pissed about it."

Charles replied, "Oh he is pissed, huh? He does not know what pissed is until I get hold of him! I will show his ass pissed."

Donna asked, "Patricia do you believe Andre would be bold enough to come after us? Is that what you are trying to say?"

Patricia said, "I am not sure because sometimes Andre gets pretty crazy."

Charles said, "You really need to get away from that crazy fool!"

"There is something else I need to tell you all," Patricia said as tears began to stream down her face again.

Everyone silently waited in anticipation to hear what Patricia had to say. As Patricia paused for a while so she could get the words out, there was a moment of silence.

She finally was able to say, "I am pregnant."

Charles said, "Patricia, you are joking, right?"

"No dad, I am very serious."

Charles said, "Well you two certainly did not waste any time!"

Nobody was too happy about the news as friends and family usually would be on such an occasion. They all knew Andre was no good for Patricia and now she was going to have a child by him. It was even clear by the way Patricia delivered the news that she was not even happy about it.

Donna said, "Patricia what were you thinking about? Certainly you could not have been thinking straight or rationally."

"Well I did not want it to happen so soon but it did. So that is where we are now. How do we know that this baby won't change Andre? Now, I am going to have Andre's baby, so can we move on?"

She could never tell them how this baby was actually conceived. She would not let them know about the vicious rapes. Andre got pleasure out of forcing her to have sex with him while he battered and abused her. Even if Patricia did not resist, Andre was still aggressive. Sometimes it seemed like he was even more aggressive when she did not fight. Patricia was just never in the mood for Andre. He no longer turned her on. He felt he had the right to take that part of her because he believed she was his property.

Charles said, "Andre is going to be a part of you and that baby's life in some way for a long time."

Patricia was overwhelmed with emotion and hurt as she said, "Look I am real confused now so can I just have a moment alone? Please!"

Charles stood up and said, "Okay everybody, let's give her some space."

Charles escorted Yvette and Vanessa to the door. Patricia lies on the couch and begins to cry out loudly. Charles and Donna try to console her at first but then they walk away and allow her to get everything out.

CHAPTER TWENTY-THREE

****

Patricia went back home but she was reluctant to go inside. In fact, she waited outside for over an hour trying to get the courage to face Andre. She noticed the beer boxes and bottles outside in the trash. It actually appeared as if Andre had a party but that was not the case. He had been drinking heavily.

Patricia had hoped perhaps he was fast asleep from his alcohol consumption. It was getting late and Patricia was getting tired of waiting outside. She knew she had few choices. She could sleep outside; go to crazy Vanessa's house or go to her somewhat worrisome parent's house. Yvette's house or a battered woman's shelter was definitely out of the question.

She chose to risk a beating and go inside. She quietly opened the front door and began tip-toeing through the house. She carried a small flashlight with her which she used to sneak through the house.

Andre slept pretty hard when he drank. However, turning on the lights would usually wake him.

Andre was passed out on the couch in his usual spot, with his work clothes still on. Emptied beer bottles littered the coffee table. He appeared to be waking up, so Patricia stopped dead in her tracks and froze. She waited for Andre to stop moving around and then she continued to the bedroom. She felt once again she avoided a confrontation with Andre. Sometimes she preferred him drunk like that. He usually was too drunk to rape her or beat her up.

She was really beginning to get burned out physically and psychologically. Basically she was stressed out to the point she was tripping. She was scared to death of Andre but she was more afraid to make a move. She was afraid to come home to Andre or to just go home period. It just did not feel like home. It felt more like hell and Andre was the Devil.

Patricia was in the bed sleeping when she heard things being thrown around and broken. Andre had woken up and went on a rampage. Patricia just laid there for a while, hoping he would stop and go back to sleep. It was about one-thirty in the morning and Andre was supposed to be up for work in less than four hours. Patricia was afraid to go out there and confront Andre. She got her cell phone ready in case she had to call the police. She was hoping it did not get to that point but she certainly wanted to be ready.

Andre did manage to work his way to the back room where Patricia was. Patricia had already started getting ready to leave. Her bag was already packed because she stayed ready for these confrontations. Patricia hoped she could just get out of there with no problems.

Andre grabbed Patricia and punched her like she was a man. Patricia went down and Andre started kicking and beating her.

Andre yelled, "I am going to teach you a lesson because you are a no good bitch and you don't listen to me!"

Patricia went motionless as she lies there on the floor. Andre attempts to awaken Patricia but she does not move.

Suddenly there is a loud knock at the door. There are two black female officers standing on the outside with their hands ready on their weapons. Officer Powell is about five foot nine, thirty-two and tough looking. Officer McNeil is the less rugged looking of the two. She is about twenty-eight and about five foot six. She was smaller than Officer Powell but she was just as tough.

Andre yelled, "Who is it?"

Officer McNeil yelled, "It's the police! Now open the door before we have to open it for you!"

Andre slowly opened the door and said, "What is the problem officer? We did not call the police."

Officer McNeil wanted to make sure Andre knew exactly who they were because they were actually in plain clothes.

She said, "First of all I am Officer McNeil and this is my partner Officer Powell. We are from the DVTF unit or Domestic Violence Task Force. We are here because your neighbors called about a four-fifteen here."

Andre asked, "What the hell is a four-fifteen?"

He knew exactly what a four-fifteen was but he was just playing dumb. He never had a female officer duo arrest him, so he felt he could get over on them. After all, he was used to being in control when it came to women.

Officer Powell asked, "Are you having a fight with your wife again Mr. Robinson?"

Officer McNeil heard a faint women's cry coming from the back room as she walks down the long hallway. She rushes into the bedroom and sees Patricia on the floor.

Officer McNeil yelled out to Officer Powell, "Hook him up! We have a female down back here!"

Officer McNeil assessed Patricia's condition and said, "Ma'am I need for you to stay still. Help is coming."

She got on her two-way radio and said, "Dispatch this is Officer McNeil, roll rescue to this location for a female down. Advise response to be code three. Roll a black-and-white to this location also for transport of one male suspect. Stand by for our status. Officer Powell do you need assistance on the arrest?"

Officer Powell said, "No I am good. I can handle it."

Officer McNeil knew Officer Powell could handle herself very well. She just thought she would ask anyway. Back in the living room, Andre has taken somewhat of a fighting stance towards Officer Powell.

Officer Powell yelled at Andre, "Turn around and put your hands on your head! Do it now because that is the only warning you will get!"

Andre started slowly walking towards Officer Powell with his fists up and said, "You don't have the right to be in my house so get your partner and get the fuck out of here bitch before I have to show both of you who is in charge here. This is my house damn it and I run things here!"

Andre throws a punch at Officer Powell which was a huge mistake. Officer Powell is definitely not Patricia. Officer Powell grabbed

Andre's arm and does a Judo expert type take down. Andre hit the floor hard. She rolled Andre over, put her knee in his back and handcuffed him.

Officer McNeil has heard the commotion and pretty much knew what happened. She asked, "Is the suspect okay or do we need to double-up on rescue transport?"

Officer Powell responds, "Negative on the second rescue unit. Advise dispatch our status is code four at this location with one in custody."

She stands Andre up and says, "Perhaps you needed a lesson on how to treat women. More importantly, you better know which one you are stepping to. I am not your wife!"

Andre still struggles and said, "My wife fell and I was just getting ready to call the ambulance when you all came."

Officer Powell just shook her head and said, "Yeah right and she landed on her face about a dozen times. Tell it to the judge! Right now you have the right to remain silent, so use it! Anything you say or do can be used against you in the court of law. You have the right to an attorney and to have him present during questioning. If you cannot afford an attorney, one will be appointed to you. Do you understand your rights?"

Andre said, "Yeah I understand. I think you dislocated my shoulder bitch!"

Officer Powell said, "I am not going to be too many more bitches. Now I suggest you zip it before I have to take you down again. Trust me, the first one was nothing."

Andre wisely kept his mouth shut. The Paramedics finally arrived and assisted Patricia. They are two African-American men, whose names are Brad and Roy. Both of them were in their late twenties. As Patricia was wheeled out of the house, two uniformed officers came in. One was a large black man in his late thirties. His partner was a smaller white man, about early forties. Andre was handed over to them and they escorted him out. Officer McNeil comforted Patricia as she is put inside the ambulance. A few nosey neighbors appear outside, even at that late hour. Red and blue lights illuminate the neighborhood. Andre is placed in a marked patrol car and driven away. Simultaneously, the ambulance drives up the block in the opposite direction to the hospital.

CHAPTER TWENTY-FOUR

****

Patricia has arrived at Tri-County hospital. The two Paramedics rushed Patricia down a hospital hallway and into an emergency room. Doctor Richardson and a couple of nurses were present in the emergency room.

Doctor Richardson, a middle-aged Caucasian male, checks Patricia out and asked, "How long has she been out?"

Brad replied, "She has been coming in and out of consciousness. Her vitals appear to be normal."

Doctor Richardson continued to assess Patricia's condition and asks, "What happened to her? Is this the motor vehicle accident victim?"

Roy said, "Negative this is the domestic violence victim."

Yvette and Vanessa came rushing through the hospital. Patricia managed to call them while Andre was tossing stuff around the house.

Patricia still refused to call her parents or get them involved. Yvette had made arrangements for Patricia to meet her and Vanessa out in front of her house. They were going to pretty much rescue her from

Andre, at least for the night. They did make it to Patricia's house only to see her being rolled into the ambulance. They followed the ambulance to the hospital while going through every red light. They called Patricia's parents while they were chasing the ambulance to the hospital. Therefore, it would not be too long before they arrived at the hospital. Actually, Patricia's parents lived quite close to the hospital.

Officer McNeil and Officer Powell arrived shortly thereafter and then Donna and Charles showed up. Patricia's friends are already waiting in the waiting area. They wanted to check on Patricia but they were not her immediate family. Donna and Charles rushed into the Hospital emergency room area. Donna was still in her night-clothes, slippers and robe.

"Where is Patricia Robinson?" Charles asked the receptionist.

The Receptionist, a young Caucasian female around twenty-five, asked, "Are you folks Patricia's parents?"

"Yes we are Patricia's parents," Charles replied.

The receptionist said, "Have a seat in the waiting room and I will have a doctor or nurse update you on Patricia's status."

Donna and Charles went into the waiting area where they met up with Yvette and Vanessa. After they all embraced each other for support, they all began pacing the floor along with Charles. Doctor Richardson came into the waiting area to brief Patricia's parents.

They all surround the doctor like a football team in a huddle and Charles asks, "Is she going to be okay?"

Doctor Richardson said, "We have her stabilized at this time. She got beat up pretty good so she does have bruises, contusions and a few lacerations. We are going to have to keep her overnight for further tests and evaluations."

They all tried to speak at once and the doctor said, "I can not help much if you all speak at the same time."

After there was a short moment of silence, Donna asked, "May we go back and see her?"

Doctor Richardson said, "Not until tomorrow. She needs to get some rest now, so we have her sedated. We will keep a watchful eye on her. Believe me, she is in good hands and I believe she will make a full recovery. We will let you know if we find anything that might change that statement because everything is still in the preliminary stages."

They all collectively give somewhat of a sigh of relief. They all decided to stay at the hospital and wait for any changes in Patricia's condition. None of them believed they would be able to sleep anyway until they were sure Patricia had pulled through.

Donna said, "Doctor Patricia is pregnant. Will your tests be able to determine if the baby is okay?"

"Well, we will do an ultrasound and some other tests on her but as I said it is still early now. Now, is she on any meds or allergic to any meds?"

Donna said, "No she is not taking anything and I don't believe she is allergic to anything."

"Okay folks, I need to get back to my patients. We will keep you advised," Doctor Richardson said as he walked towards the double doors leading to the emergency room treatment area.

As Doctor Richardson left, they all took seats to wait it out. Morning came quickly as they all fell asleep.

One of the black nurses came out and said, "I need to speak to the parents of Patricia Robinson."

Donna and Charles Jumped up to greet the nurse for an update on Patricia's condition Yvette and Vanessa are obviously not Patricia's parents but they jump up in unison also.

The nurse said, "She is still in pain but she is doing a lot better. You can go back and see her briefly because she is talking."

They are all lead back to Patricia's room. Patricia is sitting up in her bed. She looks pretty bad but she seems to be conscious and alert. The nurse checks to make sure Patricia is still okay.

Donna gives Patricia a pretty long hug and asked, "You okay baby?"

Patricia said, "I guess so. I feel like I been toe-to-toe with Muhammad Ali. Nurse, I need something for my pain"

The nurse replied, "I have your sedative right here. Do you want it now or after your family leaves? They will not be able to stay too long."

Patricia said, "I think I can hang on for a while."

The Nurse adjusted Patricia's pillows and said, "I will be back in about ten minutes. Patricia if you need us you can push the button. If you all want more time with her you have to come during visiting hours."

After the nurse left and Charles put things in perspective by saying, "Your fight was not with Mohammed Ali, it was with Andre Robinson."

"What are you going to do now Patricia?" Donna asked.

"I don't know. I am still afraid and confused," Patricia replied.

Charles said, "Baby we do not have to discuss the incident with you now. If you want to get some medicine for your pain and get some sleep, we can come back later."

Patricia adjusted some pillows behind her and asked, "Where is Andre?"

Charles said, "He was arrested but he will probably be out and back home before you get out of here."

Doctor Richardson came in to adjust Patricia's IV.

Patricia said, "I guess me and Andre need to try to work this out." Doctor Richardson had to do a double take. He could not believe he heard Patricia correctly. He had seen many abused women come through the emergency room and some of them did not make it.

Doctor Richardson could no longer remain silent and said, "Young lady I hate to get in your family business but I just can't stand here and listen to you without wanting to give you some sound advice. Now, I wish I could show you some pictures of abused women who come through these doors nearly every day. Some don't even make it. Do yourself and your loved ones a favor. Get out of this situation or get some help before it is too late. Things are not likely to get better, but they are more likely to get worse. Now I will step out and let you folks have some time alone with Patricia. Once again, I am sorry for butting in."

Charles said, "No, we actually appreciate your input. It was good for Patricia to hear that from your viewpoint as a doctor."

As Doctor Richardson was leaving he stopped, turned around and said, "I can help with healing your physical injuries but I can't help you with the emotional and psychological trauma you undoubtedly have. That usually runs a lot deeper than your physical trauma."

As Doctor Richardson was leaving, Officer McNeil and Officer Powell walk in. They are there to get an official statement from Patricia.

Officer Powell asked, "Doctor, Is it okay to interview Patricia quickly?"

Doctor Richardson said, "Yeah that should be okay while things are fresh in her head. She is in pain now, so please try to be brief."

Doctor Richardson left.

Officer McNeil said, "I am Officer McNeil and this is my partner Officer Powell. We are detectives from the DVTF or Domestic Violence Task Force. We are just here to get a formal statement from Patricia. It should not take too long."

Charles asked, "Is it okay for us to stay or do you need privacy to speak with Patricia?"

Officer McNeil said, "It is okay if you stay because Patricia needs a lot of support now."

Officer Powell took out a pen and small note pad and said, "Actually we wanted to ask Patricia a few questions about what happened to her so we can do our report."

Patricia said, "Well basically it was no big deal. We just had an argument and a fight. He just has some problems and sometimes he drinks too much."

Officer McNeil looked at Officer Powell and everyone else in the room, shook her head and said, "What do you mean it was no big deal? You would not be here if it were no big deal."

Patricia said, "I am not going to press charges on him if that is what you all are wanting. It will only make him angrier and then I am the one that will have to deal with him."

Charles told Patricia, "What are you talking about Patricia? This guy beat you unconscious."

Donna began to cry and said, "Patricia, please do not let this continue. Please baby, we can't stand seeing you like this. Andre is not going to stop hurting you. He has to be stopped."

Charles hugged Donna and tried to console her.

Yvette also tried to comfort Donna by hugging her and saying,

"Everything will be okay."

Patricia asked, "Is he down at County again?"

"Yes, he is probably being booked in now. From his record, you are not his first victim. It seems Mister Robinson has a history of domestic violence charges involving his other now ex-wives," Officer McNeil said.

Donna said, "No wonder he does not like to talk about them." He was beating them too."

Patricia asked, "Yeah but they are still alive, right?"
Officer Powell said, "They both are alive but what does that have to do with anything?"

Patricia said, "Well everyone seems to think Andre is going to kill me or something. Andre may need some help but he is not a killer. Maybe we should just give him the benefit of the doubt."

"Girl what did that doctor give you? It must be something that got you still tripping," Vanessa said.

Yvette and Donna looked at Vanessa like she said a bad word. Charles was not so surprised because in most cases he agreed with Vanessa's views. The two of them were actually very close in their thinking about Patricia's abuse. Neither one of them bit their tongues on the issues nor did they hesitate to say how they felt at any given time.

Officer McNeil and Officer Powell looked at each other and shrugged their shoulders. They certainly were no strangers to domestic violence situations. They were seasoned officers on the police force and on the DVTF unit.

Charles added, "By the way I believe we have more than given Andre the benefit of the doubt."

"So what happens to him now? Is he going to do time for this?" Patricia asked.

Officer McNeil said, "He will have to attend the brand new, mandatory stress and anger management course which all abuse suspects have to go through. The evidence is quite clear that he abused you. I mean he has been arrested for battering you several times already. Each time you refuse to press charges he wins and manages to take a little more from you."

Officer Powell added, "Statistically the course has a very low success rate. Most of the abusers go right back to abusing. However, the program is state mandated. The old theory of locking them all up and throwing away the key does not apply anymore. The state feels there has to be some sort of intervention or rehab for domestic violence suspects.

Sad thing is those courses are always full. It could take months for him to get in."

Patricia rolled over like she was going to sleep. She asked, "So what do you want from me?"

Officer McNeil told Patricia, "As we said before we need a statement. Please don't tell us you ran into a wall or fell. Do not waste our time by trying to insult our intelligence."

"You know what happened! Maybe I don't feel like discussing it now," Patricia declared.

Donna said, "Honey we do need to discuss this. We love you and we are concerned about you."

Patricia said, "You just do not understand. Actually, I don't think any of you understand."

Patricia pressed her service button and said, "Look I just want the doctor or nurse to come back and give me something for this pain."

Officer Powell said, "Okay Patricia, we will leave and let you get some rest."

Officer McNeil reached into her pocket and pulled out a card. She pulled out a pen and wrote the number to the National Domestic Violence Hotline.

She wrote 1-800-799-SAFE and said, "That line is available twenty-four hours. Do not hesitate to call nine-one-one if you need immediate assistance."

It was almost like Patricia was ignoring the officers as she took the card, tossed it on the night stand and asked, "So when do I get to see my husband?"

Officer Powell responded by saying, "Hopefully not before the ink dries on our reports. He is being booked on resisting arrest and attempted assault on a police officer. That should keep him behind bars quite a bit longer."

Patricia said, "Thank you officers."

She pressed the service button once again. The officers left looking sort of dejected and defeated. They felt they were not able to get through to Patricia. Patricia rolled back over, this time facing away from everyone. She assumed her favorite stress relieving position; the fetal position. She began to cry loudly.

"It's going to be alright Patricia. We are all here for you and we are going to get you through this. You just get better baby," Donna said as she rubbed on Patricia's back.

Yvette started to cry and for the first time, Vanessa was over-whelmed and started to cry. They all hugged Patricia and then left.

CHAPTER TWENTY-FIVE

****

Two weeks later it was girls' night out for Patricia, Vanessa and Yvette. They finally were getting an opportunity to hang together. They were at a nightclub called Club Elegance.

Slow music can be heard playing in the background as DJ Rob Smooth says, "I will be the host for the night representing 104.9FM, the oldies beat station."

DJ Rob Smooth looked sort of like a short Heavy D. Patricia looked kind of tense. This was mandatory fun night and Vanessa and Yvette were not going to let Patricia stay in a gloomy mood.

Vanessa said, "Girl you need to loosen up a bit. We brought you out here to have some fun and damn it you are going to have some fun!"

Patricia pulled out a portable lighted vanity mirror, looked at her face and said, "I will be okay. My face looks okay, right?"

Vanessa said, "Your face looks fine. You sure put enough make-up on. Shit, you look like the damn Joker."

Patricia was looking all around the club like she was expecting someone. She just was not sure if Andre would show up. She is clearly nervous about being out with her friends. Andre was definitely on her mind.

Vanessa said, "Girl I told you to stop tripping when you are out with us. That fool is not going to show up in here with all these potential witnesses! He would be crazy to try something. Besides, if he does, you know we got your back. You know we can't stand his trifling ass anyway."

Patricia surprises Yvette and Vanessa when she defends Andre by saying, "Vanessa I really wish you wouldn't disrespect my husband like that."

Vanessa and Yvette just sat there for a few seconds looking at Patricia with their mouths open. They just do not know what it will take to get through to her. Vanessa wanted to say something in response to what Patricia said. However, she was not going to let an argument about Andre develop and ruin their evening. Not on this special occasion.

Yvette said, "We came here to have a good time. So let's leave our baggage and relationship woes behind us and have some damn fun!"

Vanessa agreed with Yvette and said, "Yeah that is true. We came here to party so let's do this! Shit you know I am ready to get my groove on. Just look at all these fine brothers in here."

Yvette said, "I will be right back. I need to speak to DJ Rob Smooth. Remember Patricia; this is our night."

Yvette returned to the table and sat down with a big smile on her face. She knew just what would get all of them on the dance floor. It was sort of like an anthem for the girls.

As the music fades out DJ Rob Smooth says, "Don't forget to come on out and enjoy Hip-hop and reggae night here at Club Elegance every Saturday with drink specials until eleven. This next song goes out to Patricia Robinson from her best friends Yvette and Vanessa. It's called, "Lady's Night" by Kool and the Gang. This is Flash-back Friday and I am DJ Rob Smooth from FM one-zero-four point nine."

DJ Rob Smooth spins the record. Yvette and Vanessa pulled Patricia on the dance floor. The crowd opens up the dance floor like the red sea. It was as if they knew that these three sisters needed the space.

The girls do a very nice dance routine. They dance so well together it looks as if the routine was rehearsed. You can see how strong their friendship really is as Patricia is smiling and having fun. For that moment, Yvette and Vanessa had made Patricia have fun and forget about her problems with Andre.

CHAPTER TWENTY-SIX

****

Once again Patricia had gone back home to Andre. Andre sat Patricia on the couch and said, "Okay baby, now cover your eyes. No peaking."

He runs to the closet and brings out several boxes. At that point Patricia's pregnancy was quite noticeable and she was showing.

"Okay, you can open your eyes now," Andre said as he set the boxes on the couch.

"Wow honey what is all this?" Patricia asked as her eyes widened.

Andre said, "I have a few gifts for you baby. Go ahead and open them up."

Patricia hugged Andre. She tore open the box like a child on Christmas morning. The first box contained two beautiful dresses.

"Thank you baby, I love them," Patricia said as she put the dresses up to her body to see how they would look on her.

Andre said, "Then I am sure you will love the rest."

Patricia proceeded to open the next few boxes at the same time because they were obviously shoes. She received three sets of very fashionable shoes.

As Patricia began to slip on the shoes and try on each pair she said, "What is today? Did I forget some special occasion or something? I know it is not my birthday and I know it is not our anniversary."

Andre said, "No baby I just wanted to show you how much I love you."

Patricia hugged Andre again and said, "Oh Andre you are so sweet."

Patricia opened the rest of the boxes, which were considerably smaller. Those boxes contained a beautiful watch and several articles of jewelry of unspecified value.

Patricia said, "Baby I am somewhat speechless."

She gave Andre one last long hug and said, "I love everything baby. Thank you, but I feel bad because I did not get anything for you."

Andre spun Patricia around and said, "I am sure you have something I might like to have a little later tonight."

He smiled, winked, pulled Patricia close to him and said, "Maybe a little later with me, you and some Luther."

Patricia said, "Andre I am just not feeling sexual tonight."

Patricia put her hand over her mouth as if she did not want that to come out. She felt that once again she would be spoiling a perfect evening and possibly ruffling Andre's feathers.

Andre pretty much ignored Patricia's comment. He knew she would not have consensual sex with him. However, he was trying to appear to be romantic so she would forgive him again.

Andre said, "Well you don't have to cook tonight baby."

Patricia was surprised and asked, "Why baby? Aren't you hungry?"

"Yes I am starving, but tonight is a Red Lobster night. Dinner is on me."

Patricia hugged Andre, gave him a nice long kiss and said, "Thanks for everything Andre. You really made my day."

****

Patricia was at home with Andre about two months later. Andre had been quite passive to date. She was really showing big time now and she was in her third trimester. She wobbled around the kitchen picking up beer bottles. Andre was sitting at the dinner table, faced down and passed out. He had been drinking heavily. She just stood there looking at Andre for a while. She shook her head in disgust.

Patricia was tired of Andre. She planned to get out of the house away from Andre. This time she would not return. She knew it was never good news when he drank like that. She went into the closet and got her going away bag. It had pretty much most of her belongings in it. Patricia dropped her keys and Andre jumped up. Patricia had got all the way to the door and was standing there with the door open.

Andre asked, "Where the hell are you going?"

Patricia starts to shake. She did not know what to say. Her first thought was to make a run for her car, but in her condition he would probably catch up to her.

The thought of her escaping stayed in her mind. She was packed and ready to go. She had finally decided enough was enough. She had planned on leaving Andre if he threatened her or their unborn child in any way.

She had to think fast and said, "I have to go to the medical facility to get checked out. I am pregnant Andre, remember?"

Andre said, "You better bring your ass back in here girl! Don't make me come after you."

Patricia knew her escape plan would probably not work at that time. However, she felt she might be able to wait him out. After all, Andre was pretty drunk. She was hoping maybe he would fall back to sleep and she would get another opportunity to escape. She did come back in the house and place her bag right near the front door. The closet might have been too far away and would impede any escape attempt.

Andre stood up and said with slurred speech, "Yeah but how do I know it's my baby? Shit the way you been running those damn streets with them two whores makes me wonder. I have been following your ass so I know you still hang out with them. Does Club Elegance ring a fuck-ing bell?"

Once again Patricia defended her friendship with the girls by saying, "Andre I told you, we practically grew up together and…"

Andre cut Patricia off and said, "I really don't give a shit! I told you I do not want you with them but you don't want to listen to me."

Patricia said, "Andre how can you say you are not sure if you are the father? That is a terrible thing to say to me. All you have to do is count back to when you viciously attacked me and raped me."

"I never raped you bitch. You are my wife so your stuff is mine too. I can do you whenever I want you fat slut! Like I said, I know you been doing other brothers. I am not stupid. Shit, that baby might be the mailman's or the damn garbage man's for all I know!"

Patricia was at the point where she was going to leave no matter what. She knew she needed to get out of there before things got too hot. She was thinking perhaps she waited too long after all. She picked up her keys and was looking towards the door where her bag was. She was looking around for something to protect herself with. She was not going to take another beating from Andre. She felt it could jeopardize her unborn baby. However, she was not going to take his disrespectful and psychologically abusive comments. Her mindset was in "fight or flight" mode.

Patricia said, "Andre I don't have time for this. I need to go get checked out. This is important if I am going to have a healthy baby."

"I do not care about an appointment! Now sit your ass down and shut up. You are not calling the shots here," Andre said.

Patricia defiantly said, "I am getting ready to leave!"

Patricia managed to get all the way over to the door. She picked up her bag and opened the door. Andre rushed over and slammed the door, nearly taking Patricia's arm off. Patricia's eyes widen as she now knows she is in big trouble. She does not know how she can get away in her condition and she does not have a weapon to protect herself.

"Andre please don't hurt me."

Andre began pushing Patricia back towards the couch and said. "I said sit your fat ass down!"

Patricia sat on the couch. She was scared but she felt she had to talk to Andre about what has been inside her for so long. Even at the risk of getting beat by him. She was also worried about him raping her again, even in her condition.

Patricia calmly said, "Andre we need to talk."

"Talk about what?"

"Andre we need to discuss this marriage."

She thought if she was going to get a beating anyway, she was going to tell him how she felt. She thought that maybe standing up to him would empower her.

Patricia yelled, "I can't take this shit anymore! I don't know, I thought you would change, but you will never change."

Andre said, "Girl I don't know what you are talking about."

Patricia finally said, "Andre I want out of this marriage."

Andre kicked over a chair and said, "You are not going anywhere bitch. There is no place for you to run and no place for you to hide because I will find you. You are going to be my wife, "Until death do us part," just like you said in your wedding vows."

Patricia was starting to get bolder and angrier. She was prepared to fight her way out of there if she had to. She wanted to get to the kitchen so she could get a pot, pan or skillet. A butcher knife was certainly not out of the question.

Patricia said, "Andre you really need to get some help."

Andre goes into the closet and pulls out a small black bag. He sits back down on the couch right next to Patricia and places the black bag on the coffee table.

He then opens the black bag, takes out a revolver and says, "This is my help right here bitch!"

Suddenly Patricia was frightened again. She was staring at Andre, who was not very stable, with a gun. She not only feared for her life, but she also feared for her unborn child's life. She was beginning to think she would not live to see the next day. She wanted to at least try to calm Andre down. She felt that might be her only chance to get out of the situation. Things are not looking too good and appear to be going from bad to worse after Andre dumps some bullets out on the table.

He starts standing bullets upright on the table while saying, "You see this revolver holds six bullets. This first one is for your ugly ass. This second one is for your punk-ass father. This third one is for your bitch-ass mom. This fourth bullet is for your ugly-ass friend Yvette. This fifth bullet is for your dumb-ass friend Vanessa. Shit, I should bust two in her ass!" Andre does not put the sixth bullet aside and stand it up with the other five. Instead he loads it into the revolver and spins the chamber. He calmly asked, "Patricia you down for a little game of Russian roulette?"

Patricia replied by saying, "Andre please stop playing with that thing and put it away."

Andre ignored Patricia and said, "Last, but of course not least, this sixth bullet is for myself. That's right you fat-ass whore, I am not afraid to swallow one of these."

Patricia continued to plead with Andre and said, "Come on Andre please stop because you are really scaring me now."

Andre appeared to be on a mission and completely ignored Patricia as he puts the gun to his own head and says, "You don't think I will do myself?

Andre stands up and paces back and forth with the gun still pointed at his head. Patricia gets up and slowly walks towards Andre. She is risking her own life and the life of her unborn child to prevent Andre from blowing his head off. Andre pulls the trigger four times and there is a distinctive click each time.

Andre looks Patricia right in the eyes and says, "I got two more chances to do this. One will take my ass out."

Andre pulls the trigger one more time. Once again, fortunately there is just a click. Patricia continues to slowly walk towards Andre. She gets close enough to hold out her hand in hopes Andre will just hand the weapon over to her.

Patricia then said, "Andre please give me the gun. I love you and I don't want to lose you."

Andre pointed the weapon at Patricia and said, "Don't come any closer! This one will not just click."

Patricia wisely does what she is told. She slowly and carefully backs up.

Andre said, "You want to leave me just like those other two bitches. I know where both of them are and I planned to take them out too. I have a couple of slugs for their asses too. I think I will do them before I do myself. I made the mistake of letting them go but I am not letting you go anywhere. No way! If you go it is going to be in a body bag."

Patricia felt her best defense at this point would be to try to con Andre and to lie her way out of the situation. She was not sure any thing she said would get through to him because he was so drunk.

He continued slamming down beers even through all that was happening. He managed to hold his beer in his left hand while holding off Patricia with the revolver in his right hand.

Patricia said, "Andre I am not leaving you. I would never leave you. I told you I love you baby."

"You are lying to me bitch! Don't try to play with my mind. No other man will do what I do for you. And no other man would want your miserable fat pregnant ass. So, if you want to leave, be my guess."

"Andre I am telling you the truth, I swear."

Andre put the gun on the coffee table. He walked away from it but then paused right in his tracks. He turned around, picked the gun back up and put it in his waist band.

Andre pointed his finger at Patricia and said, "I tell you what. You want to leave me you ungrateful slut? I will go pack your shit!"

Andre left for a while and went to the bedroom. Patricia made a mad dash for the kitchen phone. She knew that the emergency services could track that number if she could not finish her call.

She dialed nine-one-one and barely above a whisper, said, "Yes I need help here because I think my husband wants to kill me... Yes his name is Andre Robinson and he has a gun... Please hurry! She hangs up and dials her parent's house. Charles answers the phone.

Patricia continues to talk low, nearly whispering and says, "Daddy Andre is at it again... Yeah, please hurry he has a gun!"

Suddenly Andre's arm reaches around the wall and pulls the cord from the phone, startling Patricia.

Andre asks, "Who the hell are you talking to?"

Patricia said, "My father Andre. I can still talk to my parents, right?"

Andre said, "Not on my phone bitch. And he better not come over here to pick you up unless he wants a cap busted in his ass. I said you are not leaving and I meant that shit."

Patricia said, "Andre I am a little confused now. I thought you said you were packing up my shit so I can leave."

Andre slammed down another beer and said, "I changed my mind so go sit your ass down."

Patricia was really hoping Andre would have let her go. Now she felt she could become Andre's hostage. The police were definitely on the way and she thought Andre might decide to go out in a blaze of glory. She had a bad feeling about how the whole situation would play out. She did not believe Andre would go peacefully this time. She was still thinking of a way to escape from Andre.

Andre yelled at Patricia and said, "Sit!"

Patricia quickly sat down, still looking for a weapon. She had wished she grabbed a knife or something when she went to the kitchen to call the police. However, a knife or weapon was not on her mind at that time. Besides, she would have been bringing a knife to a possible gun fight.

Andre said, "I think you forgot your most important wedding vow. Remember when you stood up there and said, "Until death do us part?" I believe in that vow. Those other two whores I married forgot about that vow and so did you."

Patricia could not sit there and listen to Andre talk trash. He kept making her more and more mad. She had planned to try to ignore him, hoping he would shut up and calm down. Usually, he did not force her to listen to him for a long period of time. For her it was worse than a beating.

Patricia looked at Andre with hatred in her eyes and said, "Andre I think you are forgetting that there are other lines that go with that vow that are equally important. I believe, in fact I know, "To love and to honor," comes before that."

"Yeah right Patricia, whatever. I said it is the most important one to me because the only thing that should separate us is death," Andre replied.

Patricia said, "Look Andre, I am tired of trying to please you. You don't appreciate anything I do for you. Sometimes you treat me like a queen and those are our best times together. Other times you treat me like shit. You are like a Doctor Jekyll and Mister Hyde. Every day I wake up I wonder which one you are going to be."

Andre said, "You need to stop watching all them damn talk shows and reading all them stupid novels. Furthermore you need to stay away from your two crazy-ass friends like I told you. They fill your head with all that crap. Your friends and your parents try to make you believe I am some sort of monster and you feed into that shit."

"Andre I am really starting to believe what everyone was saying to me all along. Not just my friends and family. I am hearing the voices of Officer McNeil, Officer Powell, Gina Perkins and Doctor Richardson, all at the same time. Andre you will never change and I will never have any peace here. I don't want the baby coming up in a volatile environment. The vicious cycle stops here!"

Andre got up and walked towards Patricia and got right in her face and said, "Shut up! If my mother talked to my father the way you are talking to me she would have been picking up her teeth. He taught me to do whatever it takes to control a woman. I used to hate when he hit on my mother, but he told me some women need discipline just like a child. Later on, when my mother fled with us, I started hating her for leaving my dad. Once I started having relationships, what he told me started making sense. Maybe these nightmares are him talking to me from the grave. Shit, my father was right all along."

"So basically your father taught you to abuse women, right?" Patricia asked.

Andre replied, "That's right! He kicked my ass often too to toughen me up. He said I was not going to be a punk because no Robinson has ever been a punk. He also said if I could not control a woman by any means necessary I am less than a man."

Patricia believed things would turn for the better if she could keep on talking with him. She just wanted to watch what she said to him. At this point in the relationship she pretty much knew most of the things that set him off.

There were times when a good argument from Patricia actually calmed Andre down. He would get the opportunity to verbally vent or in actuality verbally abuse Patricia. Patricia had learned that sometimes if she out-argued Andre he would simply leave here alone. This course of action was certainly not without risks. On some occasions, the argument would escalate and get to the physical level. She knew if she could engage Andre for just a little while longer the police would be there.

Patricia said, "Andre you really need some help badly and I doubt you are going to get it from that stupid anger management course."

"You better not tell me what I need bitch! I need a damn obedient wife," Andre declared.

Patricia said, "Andre I called the police and my father and they are on the way."

She thought maybe if Andre knew the police were on the way he might calm down and not do something stupid.

Andre said, "Big deal, you called the police. I will be right back out and your dumb ugly ass will be right here waiting for me, just like always. I told you nobody else wants you and you know it."

Patricia said, "Not this time Andre. I am pressing charges on you this time. I just can't handle this anymore. I guess maybe then you can get the help you need."

Andre began pacing back and forth once again. He was clearly livid at that point. Patricia knew she had gotten to him. He was very upset but he still had not physically attacked Patricia. Patricia was confident she would be able to get out of this in one piece. She was wondering where the Calvary was and when they would show up. The problem she saw was Andre still had the gun in his waist. He took the gun out, loaded it and then put it back in his waste band. There were still plenty of bullets on the table so Patricia's thoughts of Andre going out in a blaze of glory were beginning to look like a reality.

"You will pay for all the shit you put me through. I can assure you of that you fat bitch," Andre said as he continued to pace the floor.

Patricia was shocked that Andre would believe she put him through hell, so she said, "Andre the shit I put you through?"

Andre said, "Yeah you heard me you ungrateful fat whore!"

Patricia had heard enough and refused to let Andre think he broke her. She boldly stood up and said, "I will not live in fear of you Andre. Moreover, I am not a bitch, whore or any of the negative terms you address me as. I am a strong and beautiful black woman. Now, I am going to wait for the police to get here and I am going to gather my things and get the hell out of here. When you get out this time I will not be coming back. I don't want this anymore so I am moving on Andre."

Andre slapped Patricia back down on the couch. At this point sirens could be heard approaching the house and Patricia was relieved.

She stood back up and said, "I have taken your best shots Andre, but you have not and will not break my spirit. The Lord has taken me though all this and Andre I am still standing."

Andre grabbed Patricia by the throat and started choking her. Patricia said, barely above a whisper, "Andre I can't breathe!"

Andre only tightened his grasp and said, "I told you "until death do us part" and I meant it. So if you want to leave me, maybe I should kill your ass!"

Patricia struggled and fought to get Andre off her but she appears to be slowly fading out. Suddenly there is a loud pop. Andre loosens his grip and drops to one knee.

Andre grabs his stomach and says, "You shot me bitch."

He tries to grab Patricia again. Patricia pumps the remaining five rounds into Andre, emptying the gun. She just continues pulling the trigger as if she wanted to squeeze out some more rounds. Andre collapses. Patricia screams and jumps around with the gun still in her hand. Officer McNeil, Officer Powell and quite a few uniformed officers bust into the apartment with weapons drawn.

Officer McNeil says, "Patricia put the gun down... Please!"

Patricia wisely drops the gun and shouts, "He was going to kill me!"

Officer Powell kneeled down and checked Andre's pulse. She looked up at the other officers and shakes her head no signifying there is no pulse. She approaches Patricia with her handcuffs out and slaps them on Patricia's wrist.

Officer Powell sadly said, "Patricia I know you are pregnant but I have to do this. It is standard procedure to cuff all suspects. You have the right to remain silent; anything you say can and will be used against you in a court of law; you have the right to an attorney; if you cannot afford one, one will be appointed to you. Do you understand your rights Patricia?"

Patricia replied, "Yes, but he was going to kill me!"

Officer McNeil radioed dispatch and said, "Dispatch this is Officer McNeil of the DVTF. Roll rescue to this location for a man down with multiple gunshot wounds. Victim is unresponsive at this time and possibly a one-eighty-seven. Response is code three. We have one female suspect in custody."

They were all too familiar with Andre beating Patricia from the numerous previous calls. Usually, Patricia was the victim down. This time she was the one standing and Andre was the victim down.

After a moment of silence, the dispatcher said, "Confirming the male subject is down?"

Officer McNeil said, "That is affirmative dispatch, the male subject is down and unresponsive."

Charles arrives on the scene. He sees the yellow crime scene tape being put around the house.

Charles came charging into the house with his big stick and asked, "Did that son of a bitch hurt my daughter?"

Charles sees Andre lying on the floor in a pool of blood and says, "Oh my God, what happened?"

Patricia, in shock, continues to say, "He was going to kill me!"

Charles said, "Baby do not say anything else."

Officer McNeil and several other officers had Charles drop the stick and they started moving him rather quickly to the door.

Charles said, "Wait! Why are you arresting my daughter?"

Officer McNeil said, "Your daughter is a suspect in the shooting of Andre Robinson. Now you are welcome to come down to the station but this apartment is now officially a crime scene and therefore off-limits."

Two Paramedics rush in to attempt CPR on Andre but it is definitely too late.

CHAPTER TWENTY-EIGHT

****

We are now go back in Doctor Morgan's office, where Patricia is finally telling her traumatic story for the first time while being incarcerated. Patricia was crying like a baby and there is a mountain of used tissues piled on Doctor Morgan's desk.

"That is pretty much it. Now I am here doing time for it. I did have a baby boy since I have been incarcerated. I named him Marcus," Patricia said as she wiped her eyes.

"Where is Marcus now?" Doctor Morgan asked.

Patricia replied, "My parents have been taking care of him. They bring him here so I can see him sometimes. Now I do love Marcus Doctor Morgan, but every time I look at him I see Andre. He favors Andre a lot. He also reminds me of the vicious rapes. I never told anyone about how he was really conceived. Not even my parents. At first I did not want him to see me in here but my parents said it was important to try to establish a relationship with him. He is already starting out with no dad."

Doctor Morgan said, "How does that make you feel? I mean it seems to me that raising Marcus is going to be a big challenge, of course knowing what you went through and having him constantly reminding you about Andre."

Patricia paused a few minutes and then said, "Well I would never take my anger out on him or abuse him, that's for sure. I hope he never experiences or witnesses the violence I experienced or the violence his father obviously experienced. I will raise him right and teach him to respect women and treat women well. The vicious cycle definitely ends here."

Doctor Morgan took a tissue, wiped his forehead and asked, "How does telling your story make you feel?"

Patricia said, "Oh God Doctor Morgan it feels great. It feels like I just lifted a huge weight off my shoulders. I guess I really wanted to tell it all along but did not know how."

Doctor Morgan said, "Patricia your story was one of the more powerful ones I have heard. Do you feel there are any long-term effects from the abuse and if so what do you feel they are?"

She looked at the Doctor sort of confused and said, "Well, I do have nightmares about Andre coming after me and Marcus."

"Your nightmares are probably similar to Andre's nightmares. They may never go away."

Patricia once again gets emotional and starts crying uncontrollably. She said, "I wish they would go away. I am getting used to them though and they don't bother me as much anymore. I still feel like it was self-defense. I kind of feel like Sharon Walker in a way because Andre is gone forever and he will never put me or any other woman through this again. I just wish I did not have to be here for it. I think if the cops would have arrived sooner they would have seen Andre choking the life out of me."

Doctor Morgan scribbled some notes down and said, "I see."

Patricia was trying to peek at his notes as she asked, "So what is your assessment or should I say diagnosis of me? Am I crazy?"

Doctor Morgan responded and said, "Oh no Patricia, I think you are fine. Considering what you have been through, I think you are very strong and should be able to get through this. You just made it through the first and most important step in the program by telling your story. Now, do you feel ready to tell it to the group?"

Patricia said, "Yeah, I feel like I can tell it to the world."

Doctor Morgan said, "When would you like to tell your story? I would like you to have the opportunity to prepare for it if need be."

He looks at his calendar and said, "It looks like I will be gone a couple of days next week but I will be here Monday, Wednesday and

Friday.

Patricia thinks for a few seconds and then says, "Let's make it Monday. I do not want to wait too long."

Doctor Morgan scribbled Patricia's name on his desk calendar and asked, "Should I pencil you in or ink you in?"

Patricia asked, "What difference does it make?"

Doctor Morgan said, "Well, if I put you down to tell your story I do not want to hear that four letter word come out of your mouth."

Patricia sort of laughed and said, "I am sorry Doctor Morgan but I do curse sometimes."

Doctor Morgan remarked, "Yeah, you curse like a drunken Sailor. However, the four letter word I am talking about is even worse around here. P-A-S-S is the word I am talking about."

Patricia said, "There is no way I would pass. I am so ready to tell my story again."

CHAPTER TWENTY-NINE

****

Monday morning came rather quickly for Patricia. As Promised, Patricia did tell her story to the group. There was not a dry eye in the joint except for Doctor Morgan's. When she finished there is a long pause and you could once again hear a pin drop. Suddenly the silence is broken with applause. The women give Patricia a standing ovation.

Doctor Morgan said, "I hope you all are applauding because it was a powerful story and not because she killed Andre."

Later that day, Patricia was out in the visitors' area. Her Lawyer, an African-American female in her forties, and two black prison guards are present. The Lawyer's name is Michelle. Patricia was quite nervous because although they had similar meetings in the past, this one seemed different.

Patricia said, "I hope you have some good news for me. I am tired of being in this hell hole."

Michelle said, "I actually do have some wonderful news for you."

Patricia excitedly asked, "What is it? What is it?"

Michelle answered, "I wanted to take the opportunity to tell you that you have successfully completed this program and have been scheduled for release."

Patricia was very much speechless. She sat there with the two guards on either side of her, with her mouth wide open. She could not believe what she was hearing. Certainly she knew she was not dreaming because most of her dreams were nightmares.

Michelle continued and said, "There was also some new evidence that came up. It seems Andre liked to videotape you and him in the house. A tape was found with some of the beatings and the rapes. Ironically, he was rolling tape the night he was killed. Turns out the Precinct had the tape all along in their evidence locker. The officer who booked it in was killed in the line of duty a short time before you went on trial. Therefore, the evidence was never turned over."

Patricia stuttered but finally got the question out. She asked, "Released from the program or released from prison?"

Michelle said, "Actually you will be released from both. You have already completed the state mandated program. The incident is being called self-defense. You will be receiving a pardon from Governor Walsh. He insisted on being a part of this. Patricia you will be fully exonerated. Now, you will be receiving some more treatment slash counseling on the outside but at least you will be doing it as a free woman."

Patricia started to cry and said, "Oh my God, that is so great! Praise the Lord! Hallelujah! I can't wait to see Marcus, my two best friends and my parents."

Michelle said, "I am very proud of you. You deserve this. Congratulations."

Patricia paused for a moment and then said, "Wait a minute. You did say a tape right? Do they know if the footage turned up anywhere else, like maybe Me Tube or on-line?"

Michelle said, "There was no evidence of any other tapes or videos at this time. However, we did not know about this tape either so you never know."

Patricia was worried about that possibility but only for a few minutes. The bigger picture was she was getting ready to be released from the prison facility. That was all that mattered to Patricia. In this moment nothing can take away from that. She probably would not have cared if there was a naked picture of her on every billboard in the city. She was getting ready to go home a free woman with time served. She felt compelled to thank Doctor Morgan and Carol for helping her open up. She would actually be prepared to thank all the women in the program who told their stories.

CHAPTER THIRTY

****

Two days later Patricia was in the Evening Scope news program studio. Governor Walsh, a middle-aged Caucasian man was present. Mayor Lindsay, a middle-aged black man, was present. Doctor Morgan was present. Patricia and her Lawyer were present. Last, but certainly not least, Robert Cassidy was present. Robert was the news program host. He is a Caucasian man, about thirty-five years old.

Robert looks into the camera and says, "Good evening, I am Rob Cassidy and this is Evening Scope News Program. I have lots of guest on my panel tonight so I will get right to the intros. Tonight my guests include Governor Walsh, Doctor Morgan from Hanford Woman's Correctional facility along with two women who were just released from that facility. Their names are Patricia Robinson and Carol Witherspoon. Their Lawyer is well-know of course and her name is Michelle Thompson. And of course Mayor Lindsay, who I assume is making a cameo appearance. I guess I will start with Doctor Morgan. How successful do you feel this state mandated program will be?"

Doctor Morgan said, "I think the program has great potential. I mean it is a fairly new program for our facility so I can't give you any official numbers or statistics. That being said, it has been fairly successful in other states and facilities."

Robert Cassidy said, "What do you feel will be the key to making your program more successful than other rehab programs? We all know that many of these programs fail."

Everyone on the panel looked at Robert in shock. Perhaps going on Robert's program was not such a good idea. Robert liked controversy, which gave his program high ratings. He was known to stir up a few pots and ruffle a few feathers.

Doctor Morgan said, "Well I am sure you would agree that we cannot just lock up criminals without giving them some sort of extensive and intensive rehab. Prison alone will not address the physical and psychological trauma many of these women have endured."

Robert Cassidy said, "What do you tell skeptics like me who don't believe any program will help these criminals? Why should society live in fear of these pedophiles, rapists and serial killers you all insist on putting in these programs and releasing?"

Governor Walsh said, "Our prisons are already full. We continue to spend millions of dollars building more and more prisons. At the rate we are going, there will be twice as many prisons as schools and colleges. That puts a heavy burden on our state. We feel it is imperative that we find and incorporate programs like this into the system. Hopefully we will be able to rehabilitate and successfully return prisoners back into society."

Robert Cassidy shuffles some papers, looks over to Patricia and Carol and said, "Now you two women were tried and convicted in a court of law for taking the lives of your husbands. Now I think that is murder. Would either of you care to comment?"

Patricia cleared her throat and pulled her chair up closer to the table and said, "Yes I would like to speak on that."

"Now you are umm….Carol, right?" asked Robert.

Patricia gave Robert the meanest stare-down and said, "No it is Patricia! I would like to say that you left out one very important piece of information. They were our abusive husbands. We paid for what we did and now we are ready to move on with our lives. This program helps women like us to cope with the mental anguish and pain we feel for what happened to us. Many of us were imprisoned by our husbands for many years. In a lot of cases when a woman kills her abusive husband, it is in self-defense."

Robert pauses for a moment and then says, "Well, allow me to be the devil's advocate for a minute and ask you both that age-old question. And I know you have probably answered it or heard it on numerous other occasions. Why don't you just get out of the relationship? You know, move on."

Carol said, "It is not always that easy Mr. Cassidy."

Doctor Morgan could see that by their expressions, Carol and Patricia were getting hotter and hotter with every one of Robert's questions. Doctor Morgan knew it would not be long before Patricia went off on Robert live on National television.

He knew she would not bite her tongue for long, so he said, "There are many reasons women stay with their abusive husbands. Some believe their husbands will change. Some are psychologically brainwashed by their abusers. Many have nowhere else to go and nobody else to turn to. The psychological abuse can have life-long effects. I have seen victims whose state of mind could be compared to a shell-shocked war veteran. Those of course would not be released. In most cases, many of them would not be in the regular prison system anyway."

Governor Walsh said, "Myself, my staff and an independent civilian review board check and review the files of every inmate that has special circumstances for their release. There are some that are rejected. For instance, there was a third female who did very well in the program but was unable to be released."

Robert asked, "Why was that Governor, if I may ask?"

Governor Walsh said "It was because she specifically went back to her husband to kill him. It was premeditated murder. We are not giving women the green light to kill their partners."

Robert Cassidy started rapping the segment up and said, "I would like to thank everyone for talking with Evening Scope. I wish both of you women luck."

He then looks right into the camera and said, "In our next segment we will be talking to some high level brass from the police department. We will be discussing the issue of alleged police misconduct within the ranks and on the force. We will be right back after a commercial break, so please stay tuned."

Patricia calmly asked, "Are we off the air?"

Robert said, "We certainly are and folks that is a wrap for this segment."

Patricia, finally able to speak freely asked, "What the hell is your problem?"

Doctor Morgan knew exactly where Patricia was heading with this discussion. He shouted, "Patricia no!"

Patricia said, "Well, he just demonized us and disrespected us on national television. We already have been through enough bull...."

"Patricia!" Doctor Morgan yelled once again to prevent Patricia from completing the curse word.

"Crap!" Patricia said.

Robert Cassidy said, "Hey, I am just doing my job. Those were tough questions that needed to be asked. Now, I am sorry if I offended you but this segment is over. The network will be returning from commercial break in forty-five seconds."

Carol started pulling on Patricia's arm and said, "Come on Patricia let's just go. He isn't even worth it."

Doctor Morgan gathered his papers and said, "Yeah let's get going. We do not want any trouble."

Governor Walsh, Michelle and the Mayor walk off the set and exit the studio. Doctor Morgan walks out with Patricia and Carol. It was as if he knew it was not over between Patricia and Robert. Carol knew Patricia pretty well too. Doctor Morgan was on one side of Patricia and Carol was on the other. Suddenly Patricia turned around and headed back towards the set. She wanted to curse Robert out. Doctor Morgan and Patricia grabbed hold of Patricia and escorted her out. The police officers arrive for the next segment and are seated at the round table.

Robert Cassidy adjusted his tie and said, "I am certainly glad to see you guys. In this case a cop was around when you needed one. I thought I was going to have to call you up to the set a little sooner. I bet that one there will end up right back in prison. She needs some help."

As Doctor Morgan was leading Patricia away he said, "Patricia you have to learn to control that temper. If you don't control your temper, you are going to continue getting yourself into trouble."

Carol agreed with Doctor Morgan and said, "Yeah he is right girl. Don't be tripping so much."

CHAPTER THIRTY-ONE

****

It is about six months later. Patricia is now at a battered women's shelter. Ironically, it is the same battered women's shelter that Gina Perkins runs. This time she is there as an official spokesperson. There are about twenty or thirty women in a large room of the facility. It looks like a hospital emergency room waiting area as many of the women are in pretty bad shape. Carol is on the stage with her. Patricia's mother, father, two friends and Marcus are all in the audience to show there support for Patricia. Patricia and Carol are making there closing statements.

Patricia said, "Remember what I said tonight. Every fifteen seconds a woman is abused in this country. Domestic violence is one of the leading causes for injuries to women ages fifteen to forty-four. There are over two thousand women in prisons and correctional facilities for killing their abusive husbands. So, in many cases we believe we can't get out of an abusive relationship. Well, I am living proof that the alternative is definitely a lot worse than anything you will encounter if you leave."

Carol added, "Please do not become a statistic or victim to domestic violence. Make a change in you and your children's lives. Remember, he is not going to make a change so it will be up to you."

As the women clapped, Gina went up on the stage. As she clapped her hands she said, "Thank you two for coming out and inspiring these women. Your stories were very inspirational."

The women gave Carol and Patricia a standing ovation. They stood there clapping for several minutes. Gina raised her hand and the women stopped applauding and took their seats.

Gina continued and said, "I have good news for all of you. Patricia has been kind enough to bring us copies of her best-selling novel entitled, "Deceptive Vows." She will be at the back table to autograph copies. I read the book and it is certainly a wonderful and informative book. In fact, I think it should be required reading for all domestic violence victims."

Patricia said, "My agent told me that there are several production companies that are interested in making this book into a movie or Lifetime television program."

Again there is a standing ovation and applause. The women are treating Patricia as if she were the first lady.

Patricia continued and said, "They all want to change the title to, "A scorned woman," but I told them I actually like "Deceptive Vows" better. Hey, as long as they tell the story like the book and compensate me fairly for it, I don't care if they call it, "Shitty Vows!"

The women all think that is pretty funny. However, they know Patricia is joking.

Patricia went on to say, "No, seriously, this goes beyond the money, fame and glory. Now I do feel fortunate to have all this success. However, I still have a mission. I promised myself to stay focused and grounded, with military-like diligence towards that mission. That mission is to bring awareness to this issue and save lives. At this time I would like to introduce you to some of my friends and family. This is my father Charles, mother Donna, son Marcus and finally, my two best friends in the whole wide world Yvette and Vanessa. One other person, who I have already thanked, is Doctor Morgan. And oh yeah, of course I can not forget to thank Gina Perkins. I owe so much to all of them."

The women give Patricia and Carol one last standing ovation. Patricia, Carol and Gina make their way to the back where there was a long table and two chairs set up. There was also a box of Patricia's books. Carol does not have a book out or movie deal in the works. Patricia brought her for moral support and to assist her with the motivational speaking side of the book signing. Carol was an outstanding speaker. On the way back to the table, the women in the audience reached out to shake Patricia and Carol's hands. Many of them give Patricia and Carol hugs. Patricia sat at the table with Carol and the women all lined up to get their autographed copy of Patricia's book.

As Patricia started to autograph books Carol said, "Well gee, I sure hope I can get a book or movie deal."

Patricia said, "Maybe you will and maybe you won't. What matters most is that we stay focused on the mission we talked about tonight. No matter what status we achieve, the mission will always be the most important thing in our lives."

CHAPTER THIRTY-TWO

****

Patricia is in Hollywood at the famous Kodak Theater. It is about four months later. She steps out of a limousine dressed to kill. Charles, Donna, Marcus, Yvette, Vanessa and Carol are also there. Patricia walks on the red carpet along with various other stars and actors. She stops and looks up at the movie marquee which read, "Deceptive Vows: a film based on the novel by Patricia Robinson."

There was an all-star cast which Starred Angela Bassett, Denzel Washington, Janet Jackson and Morgan Freeman. There were numerous other big names in the movie, including Halle Berry and it was expected to be the summer's first major blockbuster. The movie would pretty much stick to Patricia's novel version. As Patricia just stands there with her family and friends tears begin to flow down her face. After all, she had been through hell and she never expected to have so much good come out of it.

Later that night Patricia was at her new beautiful home with Marcus. Marcus was having a temper tantrum on the living room floor. He was screaming, crying and refusing to eat his food. Patricia just stood there with Marcus' food, calmly and quietly for a while.

When Patricia could not take anymore she yelled, "Marcus get your little ass in here!"

Marcus threw a toy across the room and yelled, "No, I don't want to!"

Patricia threw the plate food down and it crashed to the floor. She showed her teeth like a wild animal. There is a sudden eerie silence as Marcus seemed to be frightened. He has yet to see this side of his mother. Patricia charged in the living room after Marcus. Marcus backed up until he was trapped between the closet, wall and couch. There was no escape from Patricia's bottled up rage. She struck him several times with her fists before she froze up.

Little Marcus laid there screaming in pain and holding his face. She kneeled down, held him in her arms and cried along with him. She realized at that point she was still not over her psychological trauma. All she endured has affected her and turned her into a monster. She knew and finally accepted the fact she needed further help.

FINAL THOUGHT

****

Many of the laws dealing with domestic violence changed in the nineties after the now infamous Simpson trial. There were new laws put in place to better protect the victim and give law enforcement officials more authority when investigating cases of domestic violence. A suspect can be arrested immediately if a victim shows any physical or visual signs of abuse. No questions asked.

Over recent years, more laws have been implemented, but domestic violence continues to be a major problem in today's society. If you, or someone you know, is in an abusive relationship; please contact your local law enforcement agency, social service agency or National Domestic Violence Hotline. **(1-800-799-SAFE)** It may be the difference between life and death.

********THE END********

ABOUT THE AUTHOR

Gary Tavares was born in New York on March 9, 1965. He came across rough times when he and his five brothers and sisters were abandoned by both parents. He was no older than four years old. They were all placed in a Foster home in the Bronx, New York. The six of them stayed together but Foster parents raised them. Their real parents were never located. Growing up Gary had four sets of foster parents all together. He is no stranger to abuse, as he was mentally and physically abused by his first foster parents. Fortunately, the foster agency had great social workers, counselors and child psychiatrists.

He graduated from Evander Childs High School of the Bronx, New York in 1983 at the age of eighteen. He went to the United States Navy from 1983 to 1986 and received an Honorable Discharge. He then joined the United States Army from 1986 to 1992. He received an honorable discharge from the Army also.

In 1993 Gary found out he has the gift of writing. He immediately began taking courses in creative writing to sharpen his new-found talent. At first, it was a way to channel his energy and escape the realities of life. He later decided to use this gift to educate others as well as do something positive for our communities. He started out writing educational plays. He had all four of his educational plays produced in California. He wrote, acted in and directed each play.

In 2000, he began writing Screenplays. He currently has four completed Screenplays, including Deceptive Vows (screenplay version). He is working on many others.

He started writing Poetry in 2002. He had a column in a published company newsletter. The name of the monthly newsletter was "The ATC Times". The name of the column was "Tavares' Tales". He had to write an original educational poem for the column monthly.

He has written three poetry books that address tough youth, community, political and social issues. "Inspirational and Educational Poems First Edition"(2007) "Inspirational and Educational Poems Second Edition" (2008) and "Motivational and Inspirational poems."(2010) His poem, "Battered and bruised" from his first edition, spoke about domestic violence. It won a prestigious poetry award (2007) He sent his poem entitled, "From a Dream to Reality: A Historic Election" to the Whitehouse and received an ink-pen signed "Thank you" letter with both President Obama and Michelle Obama's signature. (2009)

This novel, Deceptive Vows, was originally one of Gary's most powerful and compelling plays. He continues to use his God-given talent to educate and save lives. He is reaching out to the educational system as well as our communities with his educational genre. In 2004 Gary became a Youth Motivational Speaker. He visits schools throughout the Atlanta Georgia area. He speaks with fourth graders to high school seniors.

In November 2005, Gary established his own business in the Atlanta Georgia area. He is CEO and Founder of Tavares Entertainment, LLC. He offers creative and professional writing services as well as the development of original works.